ROUTLEDGE LIBRARY EDITIONS:
DISCOURSE ANALYSIS

Volume 8

A FORMAL APPROACH TO DISCOURSE ANAPHORA

T0394116

A FORMAL APPROACH TO DISCOURSE ANAPHORA

BONNIE LYNN WEBBER

Routledge
Taylor & Francis Group

LONDON AND NEW YORK

First published in 1979 by Garland Publishing Inc.

This edition first published in 2017
by Routledge
2 Park Square, Milton Park, Abingdon, Oxon OX14 4RN

and by Routledge
711 Third Avenue, New York, NY 10017

Routledge is an imprint of the Taylor & Francis Group, an informa business

© 1979 Bonnie Lynn Webber

British Library Cataloguing in Publication Data
A catalogue record for this book is available from the British Library

ISBN: 978-1-138-22094-2 (Set)
ISBN: 978-1-315-40146-1 (Set) (ebk)
ISBN: 978-1-138-22392-9 (Volume 8) (hbk)
ISBN: 978-1-138-22405-6 (Volume 8) (pbk)
ISBN: 978-1-315-40334-2 (Volume 8) (ebk)

Publisher's Note
The publisher has gone to great lengths to ensure the quality of this reprint but points out that some imperfections in the original copies may be apparent.

Disclaimer
The publisher has made every effort to trace copyright holders and would welcome correspondence from those they have been unable to trace.

A Formal Approach
to Discourse Anaphora

Bonnie Lynn Webber

Garland Publishing, Inc. ■ New York & London
1979

Library of Congress Cataloging in Publication Data

Webber, Bonnie Lynn.
  A formal approach to discourse anaphora.

  (Outstanding dissertations in linguistics)
  Originally presented as the author's thesis, Harvard,
1978.
  Bibliography: p.
  1. Anaphora (Linguistics)—Data processing.
2. Discourse analysis—Data processing. I. Title.
II. Series.
P299.A5W4   1979   001.6   78-67737
ISBN 0-8240-9670-3

All volumes in this series are printed on acid-free,
250-year-life paper.
Printed in the United States of America

Acknowledgements

My thanks and appreciation go out to the following people, places and things that have seen me through all or part of the past two years:

To Bill Woods, for writing more comments per page on previous versions of this manuscript than heretofore thought humanly possible.

To Ivan Sag - a good friend, a gentleman and a scholar.

To Annie Zaenen, Jorge Hankamer, Carlotta Smith, Jerry Morgan, Phil Tedeschi, Larry Horn, Polly Jacobson, Janis Williamson, Brenda Johns, Mark Liberman, Elisabet Engdahl and Edwin Williams, for making the 1977 MSSB Workshop on Discourse Grammar such a lovely month of perceptive linguistics, marvelous food and great boogie.

To Dorothy Burlage, Andee Rubin, Susan Joshi and Velma Sowers, for their support and understanding.

To Dan Kalikow, for leading me through the uncharted valleys of MRUNOFF and HTYPE.

To Wendy Gerzog and Bruce Meadows, for consenting to the use of their names in many bizarre, if not actually compromising, sentences.

To Chip Bruce, for his assurances that going bananas in the pursuit of a thesis was rarely a permanent disability.

To Jon Allen, for many words of encourangement.

To Ray Reiter, for suggesting two years ago that looking at pairs of sentences might lead to some kind of thesis topic: it did.

To Beverly Tobiason, another inveterate bargain hunter and a good friend.

To System-D, for teaching me the value of patience and fortitude.

To my parents - Natalie and Bert Gerzog, for encouragement and hugs, especially the latter.

And finally to Woody Allen, for reminding me why - "We need the eggs".

Table of Contents

Chapter 3. "One" Anaphora

Synopsis

Robust natural language man/machine communication requires a machine to have the ability to deal with anaphoric language in a perspicuous, transportable non-**ad hoc** way. That ability is critical for the extended natural language discourse required in problem solving and information seeking situations. This thesis starts from the perspective that dealing with anaphoric language can be decomposed into two complementary tasks: (1) identifying what a text potentially makes available for anaphoric reference and (2) constraining the candidate set of a given anaphoric expression down to one possible choice. In the past, it has only been the second task (usually called the "anaphor resolution" problem) that has stimulated research in psychology and artificial intelligence (AI) natural language understanding.

Such research has produced a host of interesting examples which demonstrate the range of syntactic, semantic, social and factual knowledge that can, and sometimes must, be brought to bear in choosing the intended antecedent or referent of a given anaphoric expression. It has also sugested techniques for managing that vast amount of knowledge. Unfortunately, it has also been such as to obscure the complementary task of identifying what the text makes available for anaphoric reference and how it does so. That is the focus of this thesis.

Identifying what a text makes available for anaphoric reference is not a trivial task, and in this thesis I make two strong claims:

1. None of the three types of anaphoric expressions that I have studied - definite anaphora, "one"-anaphora and verb phrase deletion - can be understood in purely linguistic terms. That is, none of them can be explained without stepping out of the language into the conceptual model each participant is synthesizing from the discourse.

2. On the other hand, if a discourse participant does not assign to each new utterance in the discourse a formal representation in which, **inter alia**,
   a. quantifiers are indicated, along with their scopes;
   b. main clauses are distinguished from relative clauses and subordinate clauses;
   c. clausal subjects are separated from clausal predicates;
   then s/he will not be able to identify all of what is being made available for anaphoric reference.

Building on these claims, I show that there is an intimate connection between such a formal sentential analysis and the synthesis of an appropriate conceptual model of the discourse.

Chapter 1 provides a background for the thesis. On the one hand, it catalogues the types of anaphoric expressions available in English, and on the other, it catalogues the types of things that can be referred to anaphorically. It reviews research on anaphor resolution in order to clarify what issues are not being treated, and concludes with a summary of the basic ideas that unify the thesis.

Those basic ideas center around the notion of a "discourse model": the speaker has a model of some situation which s/he wishes to communicate to a listener. Thus at one level, discourse is an attempt by the speaker to direct the listener in synthesizing a similar model. Informally, a discourse model is a structured collection of entities "naturally evoked" by the discourse. What is accessible to definite anaphora (definite pronouns and noun phrases) are just these "discourse entities". What is critical to deciding what a definite anaphor refers to is how these discourse entities are **described.**

Chapter 2 discusses some issues involved in synthesizing a discourse model. After considering various sources of discourse entity descriptions, a distinction is drawn between "invoking descriptions" (IDs) - ones formed solely from information in the explicit discourse - and "prior" descriptions" - ones based either on **universal** informaton about holders of a given property or fillers of a given role in a given situation or on **particular** information about an "already known" entity that a current discourse entity is presumed to map onto.

Chapter 2 focuses on the first type of description. A formal sentence-level semantic representation is proposed, motivated by the kinds of distinctions that must be drawn in constructing appropriate **IDs**. It is shown that a preliminary rule for constructing appropriate **IDs** (an "ID-rule") can then be articulated purely in terms of the structure of that representation. It is then argued that within today's technology, it is possible to form such a semantic interpretation of a sentence and identify the discourse entities it evokes. The chapter concludes with a discussion of necessary extensions to this ID-rule.

Not all anaphoric expressions refer to non-linguistic entities which inhabit discourse models. Another type, discussed in Chapter 3 under the label "one"-anaphora, comprises expressions that a speaker can use to substitute for a description (i.e., a linguistic object) s/he believes the listener to be aware of. For example,

(i) Wendy gave Ben a green tie-dyed T-shirt and Ron, a blue **one**.
one = T-shirt, tie-dyed T-shirt

The range of descriptions that both speaker and listener may have mutual access to is considered, as well as ways of providing such access to a natural language communication system. A relationship between definite anaphora and "one" anaphora is established by demonstrating that discourse entities and their descriptions make it possible to account for cases where the antecedent of a "one" anaphor is not given explicitly in the text. (Such relationships - and I have found several - point out the value of studying several types of anaphoric phenomena at once.)

Chapter 4 contains a discussion of a third type of anaphoric expression, namely verb phrase ellipsis (or deletion). Its starting point is Sag's account [1976] that verb phrase ellipsis is conditioned by "identity of predication" at the level of "logical form". This account is shown to be tenable only if one drops the notion that there is a single "logical form" for a sentence. I show how both the formal semantic representation introduced in Chapter 2 and "discourse entity" versions of it must be accessible as sources of antecedents for ellipsed verb phrases. This leads to a second consideration of sentence processing - this time, how to integrate resolving ellipsed verb phrases with resolving definite anaphora. The chapter concludes with a discussion of inference within an approach to verb phrase ellipsis.

The major portion of my research appears in Chapters 1-4. Chapter 5 contains a discussion of three areas into which this research might profitably be extended: (1) identifying the reference requirements of limited contexts; (2) exploring anaphoric reference to discourse entities evoked by sentences and larger units of text and (3) integrating the data-driven aspects of model synthesis discussed here and expectation-driven aspects, often discussed in the context of "frames", "scripts", etc.

TABLE OF CONTENTS

CHAPTER 1. Introduction

1. Statement of the Problem

This thesis follows from a desire to make natural language man/machine communication more robust, by providing an ability to deal with anaphoric language in a perspicuous, transportable non-**ad hoc** way. Without such an ability, there is no hope for the extended natural language discourse required in problem solving and information seeking situations. This thesis starts from the perspective that dealing with anaphoric language can be decomposed into two complementary tasks: (1) identifying what a text potentially makes available for anaphoric reference and (2) constraining the candidate set of a given anaphoric expression down to one possible choice. In the past however, it has only been the second of the two (usually called the "anaphor resolution" problem) that has stimulated research in psychology and artificial intelligence (AI) natural language understanding.

This research in psychology and AI has produced a host of interesting examples which demonstrate the range of syntactic, semantic, social and factual knowledge that may be critical in choosing among the possible antecedents or referents for a given anaphoric expression (or alternatively, in predisposing the listener to one particular candidate). These examples have also served to demonstrate techniques for constraining that choice to only the most probable candidate(s) or creating a predisposition towards it. (I shall have more to say about this in Section 3.2.) Unfortunately, these examples have also been such as to obscure the other problem I mentioned above - that of identifying what the text makes available for anaphoric reference and how it does so. That is the focus of this thesis.

The ability to identify what the text makes available for anaphoric reference is not a trivial one, and in this thesis I will make two strong claims:

1. None of the three types of anaphoric expressions that I have studied - definite anaphora, "one"-anaphora and verb phrase deletion - can be understood in purely linguistic terms. That is, none of them can be explained without stepping out of the

language into the conceptual model each discourse participant
is synthesizing from the discourse.

2. On the other hand, if a discourse participant does not assign
each new utterance in the discourse a formal representation in
which, **inter alia,**
   a. quantifiers are indicated, along with their scopes;
   b. main clauses are distinguished from relative clauses and
      subordinate clauses;
   c. clausal subjects are separated from clausal predicates;
   (cf. Chapter 2, Section 2; Chapter 3, Section 2; Chapter 4,
   Section 2), then that discourse participant cannot identify
   all of what is being made available for anaphoric reference.

In either case - i.e., if either the form of the discourse sentences or

the conceptual discourse model is ignored - there will be anaphoric

expressions which cannot be resolved correctly. The reason is that that

which is to serve as the intended antecedent or referent of that anaphor

was never recognized in the first place.

2. The Range of Discourse Anaphora

In the next section (Section 3), I will be surveying significant
previous research on discourse anaphora. However, in order to set this
background material itself into perspective **vis a vis** the broad extent
of the phenomenon, this section lists the types of discourse anaphora
which linguists have catalogued to date.

a. **Definite Pronoun Anaphora**

"Today I met a man with two heads. I found **him** very strange.
him = the just-mentioned man with two heads whom I met
         today

b. **Definite Noun Phrase Anaphora**

"Today I met a man who owned two talented monkeys. **The
monkeys** were discussing Proust."
the monkeys = the two just-mentioned monkeys owned by the
                just-mentioned man with two heads I met today

c. **"One(s)" Anaphora**

"Wendy got a blue crayon for her birthday and I got a purple
one."
one = crayon

d. **Verb Phrase Deletion** <*1>

<*1>. This has also been called "Verb Phrase Ellipsis", a name which I
shall be using to avoid taking a stand on whether it is what linguists
consider a deletion phenomenon.

"Whenever Wendy buys herself a new hat, Phyllis does **0** too."
0 = buy herself a new hat

e. **"Do it" Anaphora**

"Although the cat had to be taken to the vet, Wendy refused to **do it.**"
do it = take the cat to the vet

f. **"Do so" Anaphora**

"If you won't take the cat to be spayed, I will **do so.**"
do so = take the cat to be spayed

g. **Null Complement Anaphora** [Hankamer & Sag, 1976]

"Although the cat had to be taken to the vet, Wendy refused **0.**
0 = to take the cat to the vet

h. **"Sentential It" Anaphora**

"Although Marilyn's cat ate a hole in Fred's coat, **it** didn't bother him.
it = the fact that Marilyn's cat ate a hole in Fred's
        coat

"When did Marilyn's cat eat a hole in Fred's coat? I think **it** happened on New Year's Eve."
it = the event in which Marilyn's cat ate a hole in
        Fred's coat

i. **"Sluicing"** [Ross, 1969]

"Someone asked after you, but I don't remember who **0.**"
0 = asked after you

"John attended MIT, but I don't remember when **0.**"
0 = John attended MIT

j. **"Gapping"** [Ross, 1967]

"Bruce eats cottage cheese on Wednesdays, and Harry **0**, on Thursdays."
0 = eats cottage cheese

k. **"Stripping"** [Hankamer, 1971]

"Wendy eats half sour pickles, but 0_1 not 0_2 in her own apartment."
0_1 = Wendy (does)
0_2 = eat half sour pickles

l. **"Such" Anaphora**

"When Mary kicked her cat, she was punished since **such behavior** is deplorable in little girls."
such behavior =? kicking one's cat, kicking pets,
                    attacking small animals, ???

3. Historical Background

As I mentioned in Section 1, the problem of anaphor resolution -
i.e., choosing the correct antecedent or referent from among several
possible candidates - has received a great deal of attention in
artificial intelligence, most of it directed at resolving definite
anaphora (definite pronouns and definite noun phrases). One practical
reason for the general interest in dealing with anaphora arises from
wanting to provide comfortable and "habitable" [Watt, 1968] natural
language man/machine communication over a typewriter channel. If a
person is forced to make explicit what would normally be ellipsed in
communicating with another human being, s/he may find the dialogue too
time-consuming and burdensome to be of benefit, especially given the
additional burden of written rather than spoken communication. Moreover
as [Balzer et al., 1977] point out, making such information explicit is
liable to lead to more errors due to the extensive bookkeeping involved
in keeping referring expressions consistent and complete.

An additional reason for this concern with anaphora is that for
definite anaphora, there is no practical substitute in natural language.
Naming, the alternative used in both mathematics, logic and programming,
e.g.

"Let G be a barber who shaves everyone who does not shave himself."
(SETQ MYLIST (MAPCAR S (...)))

has the disadvantage of requiring the speaker to know a **priori** what will
be talked about later so that s/he can assign it a name right off. This
is impractical, if not impossible, in natural language discourse,
whether between people or between a person and a machine.

Anaphor resolution has received a significant amount of attention
from both linguists and psychologists as well. The former have looked
at it primarily in terms of "co-reference restrictions" - structural
constraints within a sentence that prevent two noun phrases from being
interpreted as referring to the same thing. Psychologists, on the other
hand, have looked at anaphor resolution in terms of memory and
processing strategies. They hope to characterize people's behavior **vis
a vis** anaphor resolution and then use that characterization in turn as

evidence for how discourse information is organized and accessed in memory. Again this work has primarily involved definite anaphora.

In order to give the reader a feeling for this research on definite anaphora, in the next section (Section 3.1) I shall present a short piece of text containing several anaphoric expressions. For each one, I shall describe various factors that have been proposed as applicable to its correct resolution. In the following section (Section 3.2), I will discuss some techniques that have been proposed by AI researchers for simplifying anaphor resolution - i.e., for predisposing the listener to one particular candidate or for constraining the reasoning that might be necessary for choosing among several possible candidates. I shall also point out that none of these techniques addresses the complementary problem I mentioned earlier - that of identifying what the text makes available for anaphoric reference. Finally in Section 3.3, I shall briefly describe the hitherto most adequate approach to verb phrase ellipsis and its remaining deficiencies that the approach to verb phrase ellipsis presented here attempts to address.

3.1 Factors Influencing Anaphor Resolution

This section is organized around a short piece of text containing several anaphoric expressions. After presenting the text, I shall describe various factors that have been proposed as applicable to the correct resolution of each expression. In many cases, the examples may not seem to justify hypothesizing these factors as an appropriate level of explanation. So interested readers are advised to consult the original sources referenced here in order to discover the range of phenomena each is meant to account for.

(a) Fred left **his** niece at home and headed for the zoo with Mary and John.
(b) Since the zoo was far away, **they** first asked a man down the block who owned a car whether **they** could borrow **it**.
(c) When **they** got to the zoo, Fred heard that a black mamba had just escaped.
(d) Suddenly near John he saw **the snake**.
(e) **The girl** saw **it** too, as did John.
(f) Fred admired John because **he** was able to catch **the snake**.
(g) Fred regretted not having a stick, since **he** could have used **it** to help John.

(h) Luckily, **the friends** had each brought a bottle of wine.
(i) John volunteered to drink **them** all in order to forget **the black mamba**.

3.1.1 Number/gender agreement

One simple factor influencing the choice of an referent for "they", "he", "it", etc. is that in English, most pronouns are marked for number and gender. So in sentences (b), (c) and (i), "they" must refer to something interpretable as a set of more than one item, while in (a), (d), (f) and (g) "he" must refer to an animate entity which is not explicitly marked "female". (That "they" is taken to refer to Fred, Mary and John in sentence (b) would result from deriving such a set using the knowledge that if x does something with y and z, one may construct a referenceable set consisting of x,y and z.)

3.1.2 Backwards Anaphora Constraint

In sentence (d), that "he" refers to Fred and not to John could be accounted for in a variety of ways that have been discussed in the linguistics literature. First, one could invoke a syntactic constraint - usually termed a "Backward Anaphor Constraint" - blocking John from being the referent of "he" based on relative depth of syntactic embedding and left-right ordering. This has been rendered in various forms in the literature by Langacker [1966], Postal [1966], Ross [1967], Culicover [1976], Reinhart [1976] and Wasow [1972].

3.1.3 Theme

A second way of accounting for Fred's being the referent of "he" in sentence (d) would be to invoke Kuno's notion of **theme** [Kuno, 1976]. According to this explanation, Fred is the theme of the discourse by virtue of being the subject of its opening sentence. The theme then is most easily pronominalizable, being what the reader is most conscious of. Hence Fred is most likely to be the referent of "he".

3.1.4 Role Inertia

A third explanation for Fred's being the referent of "he" in sentence (d) would draw upon research done by Maratsos [1973], who characterized children's performance in interpreting pronouns in terms of a simple cognitive strategy in which the roles of the participants in a discourse are changed as little as possible. According to this "inertial" explanation, since Fred is in the subject role in the previous sentence the reader will interpret subsequent sentences, if possible, with him in that same role.

3.1.5 Semantic Sectional Restrictions

In sentence (b), that "it" refers to the car owned by the man down the block whom John, Fred and Mary sought a car from, and not to either Fred's home or the zoo, may be explained on semantic or factual grounds, that a car is more likely to be the object of a borrowing than a house or a zoo. Similarly in sentence (i), the bottles of wine which the friends brought is more likely to be the referent of "them" than the friends themselves, since wine (and by extension, bottles of wine) are more likely to be drinkables than people are. Such knowledge has often been frozen into constraints called **semantic selectional restrictions**. These have been incorporated into several computer-based natural language understanding systems to aid in resolving anaphora [Burton 1976; Grosz 1977; Wilks 1975; Winograd 1972; Woods et al. 1972].

3.1.6 Recency and Scene Shifts

In sentence (e), "the girl" is understood as referring to Mary, even though two girls have been mentioned, Mary and Fred's niece. **Recency** - Mary being the last female mentioned - might be one factor influencing this assignment. Chafe [1976], speculating on what causes an item to leave someone's **consciousness**, which he views as the realm of items which can be referenced pronominally or with reduced stress, proposes that **change of scene** may remove an item from pronominal access. This seems to be substantiated by two somewhat different studies. Recent work by Grosz [1977] has shown that in task-oriented dialogues, whose structure closely parallels that of the task being performed, the participants' consciousness of an item is strongly influenced by the task structure. For example, she noticed that pronominal reference did not cross sub-task boundaries, which are essentially changes of scene. (However, Grosz does note several instances of pronominal reference skipping over whole pieces of dialogue, in cases where both sides of the intervening segment were actually part of the same sub-task.)

Also substantiating Chafe's speculation is a survey of the use of "discourse links" in newspaper articles done by Rosenberg (1976). After charting the thematic structure of several articles from the New York Times, Rosenberg notes that in his sample there were no instances of pronominal reference which crossed thematic boundaries. Even though his sample was small, it is probably the case that such cross-overs really are rare.

Explaining the preference for Mary as an antecedent in terms of change of scene, it is clear that of the two females mentioned, only Mary participates in the park scene. (Note that the fact that Mary is a girl, rather than say a woman, falls out of the anaphor-referent assignment: it is not known for certain a **priori**. If sentence (e) had been "The woman saw it too", Mary would still have been assumed to be the referent, and the fact that she was a woman would have fallen out. A similar thing is true in sentence (h), where resolving "the friends" against the set - John, Mary and Fred - provides the new information that they are friends (at least, that this is an appropriate description according to the author). This issue of anaphor resolution resulting in a further characterization of a known entity is discussed at length in [Rieger 1974].)

3.1.7 Implicit Causality

In sentence (f), "he" would normally be understood as referring to John. This cannot be the result of syntactic factors or recency because in similar sentences such as

1. Fred phoned John because he needed help.

"he" would probably be understood as referring to Fred. One way of accounting for this predisposition is to attribute it to a factor called **implicit causality** (cf. Garvey et al. [1974]; Caramazza et al. [1977]). This factor operates similarly to Maratsos' strategy mentioned above, in which anaphora are resolved so as to keep role assignments (subject, object, etc.) fixed. In the case of implicit causality, there is a bias towards resolving a definite anaphor in the subject of an embedded "because clause" toward the candidate primarily responsible for instigating the action or state denoted by the matrix clause. In sentence (f), John would be held responsible for Fred's admiration, while in sentence 1, Fred would be responsible for the phone call.

Experiments on implicit causality have shown that people resolve anaphora faster when the embedded clause is consistent with the implicit causality attributable to the matrix [Caramazza et al. 1977]. However, experiments have also shown that implicit causality is only a bias, which may be cancelled by the predicate of the embedded clause or attenuated by such factors as passivization of the matrix (which overtly marks the surface subject noun phrase as the topic of the sentence), negation (which alters the sense of causality), and the relative status of the candidates [Garvey et al. 1974].

3.1.8 Possible Worlds

In sentence (g), the referent of "it" can be described as the stick Fred would have in the set of possible worlds in which he had one. (Fred's regretting that he doesn't have a stick implies that he doesn't have one. That is, "regret" is a factive verb.) Thus, "it" refers to an entity which does not exist is Fred's "real" world. However, the clause in which "it" occurs may also be understood as referring to that same set of possible worlds. (This would not be the case if "it" occurred in a sentence like "He used it to bash the snake", which would require the antecedent of "it" to exist in the current world.) Different possible worlds are associated with different hypothetical contexts (future and modal worlds), as well as different peoples' beliefs and desires. **Possible worlds** as a factor influencing anaphor-antecedent assignments is discussed in [Karttunen 1976; Kuno 1970; Lakoff 1970].

The above short text does not provide a framework for discussing all of the factors which have been proposed to account for antecedent preferences. Other factors include emphatic stress [Akmajian and Jackendoff, 1970] and empathy [Kuno 1975, 1976]. With all these factors hypothesized as influencing anaphor-antecedent assignments, it is important to note that no one has tried to model how these factors might interact in human anaphor resolution.

3.2 Methods of Simplifying Anaphor Resolution

As should be clear from the previous section, there is a great deal of information which can be brought to bear in the process of choosing the referent of a definite anaphor. Most AI research to date in this area has involved methods of simplifying that process. In this section, I will briefly review some of these methods and show that, independent of their value in anaphor resolution, none of them addresses the complementary problem I mentioned earlier - that of identifying what the text makes available for anaphoric reference in the first place.

One significant early proposal was made by Charniak [1972]. Charniak observes that very sophisticated deductions are often needed in understanding and answering questions about children's stories. However, he also observes that in the process of making these otherwise needed deductions, anaphoric references can often be resolved at no extra cost. One example Charniak gives is the following.

> Today was Jack's birthday. Penny and Janet went to the store. They were going to get presents. Janet decided to get a top. "Don't do that" said Penny. "Jack has a top. He will make you take it back."

Charniak argues that deductions such as "If X is going to get a present and it is Y's birthday, the present is probably for Y", "If Y has a Z, s/he may not want another Z", "If Y does not want W, s/he may reject W in some way", etc. are necessary to understand this story. However, by deducing that Jack may not want another top and thus may reject one presented to him, it follows that the "it" in the final sentence of the

above example refers to the birthday present top, as opposed to the top
Jack already has. In Charniak's system, such (forward) deductions are
set up as "demons" by earlier sentences, waiting for a pattern in the
input against which they could be matched. If the matching input
pattern by chance contains an anaphoric expression, the anaphor will be
resolved by virtue of the match.

Now whatever strengths or weaknesses Charniak's demon-based system
may have **vis a vis** story understanding <*2> it is still the case that
it circumvents the complementary reference problem I mentioned above by
working, not from English, but from an internal representation
convenient for making deductions. In this representation, distinct
objects have already been assigned distinct names. For example, the
sentence "Jack has a top" is represented as (HAVE JACK1 TOP1), where
TOP1 is the distinct name for the top associated with Jack (JACK1, so as
not to be confused with any other Jack). The problem of how to go from
that sentence, uttered by Penny, to an object uniquely characterizable
as "the top that Penny said that Jack has" (or assuming one believes
Penny, as "the top that Jack has") or how to go from the remainder of
the story to another object uniquely describable as "the top that Janet
would have bought if she had bought a top" is just not considered.

Another serious effort along the lines of using forward deductions
from the previous text to simplify anaphor resolution is that of
[Rieger, 1974]. However, whereas Charniak resolves an anaphoric
expression in parallel with matching the pattern of one of his highly
particularized forward deductions, Rieger only assumes that the
"spontaneous" probabilistic forward deductions made by his system will
be useful in constraining, if not completely resolving a referring
expression.

-      The particular example that Rieger gives of reference resolution is
the following. <*3>

<*2>. [Charniak, 1975] points out some of its deficiencies.
<*3>. Although this example involves resolving a first name, it can
easily be reworked in terms of a more obvious kind of definite anaphor.

2. Andy's diaper is wet.

Rieger considers a memory space containing two tokens, one whose "descriptive set" (i.e., property list) contains the information that its real world counterpart is a person whose first name is Andy, who is 16 months old, etc., the other whose descriptive set says that its counterpart is a person whose first name is Andy, who is 25 years old, who attends Stanford, etc. Rieger then considers the problem of which of these memory tokens - i.e., their counterparts - the "Andy" in sentence 2 refers to. He shows how the "spontaneous" deduction that this Andy is probably an infant - i.e., is under 2 years old - introduces an assertion which is in conflict with the assertion that Andy is 25 years old. Thus "Andy" probably refers to the Andy who is 16-month old instead.

As far as how tokens get into memory along with an appropriate descriptive set, Rieger touches upon this problem only slightly. In particular, he sketches how memory processes would respond differently to the two simple sentences "John gave Mary a book about whales" (indefinite singular) versus "John gave Mary the book about whales" (definite singular). In the first case, a new memory token would be created with a descriptive set indicating that its counterpart was a book, was about whales and was what John gave to Mary. In the second case, an already existing memory token would be sought. However Rieger goes no further than this cursory discussion of simple singular terms and their associated memory tokens. However, this is what I shall do in Chapter 2, by considering in detail the memory tokens (which I call "discourse entities", cf. Section 5) associated with both definite and indefinite terms, plural as well as singular, and the effects due to quantifier and structural dependencies in all four cases.

Other attempts at simplifying anaphor resolution have used more organized high-level expectations than either Charniak or Rieger. In particular, Grosz [1977] shows how, in task-oriented dialogues, the structure of the task in terms of a hierarchy of sub-tasks can be used to simplify the problem. That is, she argues that the referent of a definite anaphor must be within the current context, where "current context" is defined by the current sub-task. Similarly, Bullwinkle [1977] discusses how identifying the intent of an utterance (i.e., its "speech act" [Searle, 1969]) and its role in the overall discourse (what she calls "speech act interpretation") can be used, in effect, to delimit the current context and hence constrain the referent of a definite anaphor. To this same end, Hobbs [1976a&b] uses an incrementally growing "discourse structure" derived from the text, which indicates explicitly the relations between its sentences (e.g. temporal succession, cause, contrast, paraphrase, etc.).

These attempts to constrain the possible referents of an anaphoric expression by identifying and then searching only the current context seem to me intuitively on the right track. However, the complementary problem, as I see it, still remains - that of identifying the inhabitants of that context. This is the problem which I try in part to address.

3.3 Previous Research on Verb Phrase Ellipsis

Verb phrase ellipsis has been classified by some linguists [Hankamer & Sag, 1976] as a type of "surface anaphora". "Surface anaphora" are so called because they are seen to be purely surface phenomena. The primary condition Hankamer & Sag give for a successful surface anaphor-antecedent pair is that the antecedent forms a coherent structural unit at the level of surface syntax or the level of logical form (subject to some type of Backward Anaphor Constraint, cf. Section 3.1.2). However, that condition is not fulfilled in all instances of verb phrase ellipsis. <*4>

3a. I can walk and I can chew gum.
 b. Ford can 0 too, but not at the same time.
    0 = walk and chew gum
 4. China is a country that Nixon wants to visit, and he will 0 too, if he gets an invitation soon.
    0 = visit China

<*4>. Similar examples can be given for other types of surface anaphora, cf. [Nash-Webber, 1977].

5a. A little boy I met asked me to tie his shoe laces.
 b. Although I was surprised, I did **0**.
    0 = tie that little boy's shoe laces

The problem is that of accounting for such exceptions to the above constraint on surface anaphor-antecedent pairs.

Now if such examples are ignored, the approach to verb phrase ellipsis or deletion (VPD) presented in Sag [1976] seems to account for a wide range of the remaining data. Sag's thesis is that verb phrase ellipsis is conditioned by identical predicates (rather than by identical VPs or identical substrings) in a logical form representation of the two clauses involved. (Identity here is determined modulo differences in the names of bound variables, i.e., "alphabetic variance".) This logical form representation makes essential use of the abstraction operator (λ) both to bind variables and to form complex predicates which may themselves contain quantifiers and logical connectives. For example, Sag assigns the sentence "John scratched his arm" the two logical form representations

a. John$_i$, $\lambda(x)(x$ scratched his$_i$ arm)
b. John$_i$, $\lambda(x)(x$ scratched x's arm)

That there are two possible logical forms for this sentence explains the ambiguity to be found in a subsequent ellipsed verb phrase sentence like

Fred did **0** too.

(Did what? Scratched his own arm or scratched John's?) Sag claims that

> With respect to a sentence S, VPD can delete any VP in S whose representation at the level of logical form is a lambda-expression that is an alphabetic variant of another lambda-expression present in the logical form of S or in the logical form of some other sentence S' which precedes S in the discourse.

In short, Sag shows that by looking at sentences in terms of the predicate-argument relations they express, a clean account can be given of verb phrase ellipsis (barring the set of examples given above). This in turn gives credence to the psychological reality of some type of "logical representation" within the dual processes of text generation and comprehension.

But if the process of forming a logical representation is part of the normal process of understanding discourse, then it is possible that **alternative** ways of understanding a sentence or sequence of sentences or even valid, salient **implications** of sentences may also provide lambda-predicates for verb phrase ellipsis. Thus the approach to verb phrase ellipsis presented in Chapter 4, while based on similar notions of "identity of predication" also embodies my feeling that for such an approach to be adequate, it cannot be constructed in isolation from other aspects of sentence understanding, including the identification of discourse entities discussed in Chapter 2.

(Verb phrase ellipsis, as such, has not been treated in any AI system that I am aware of. In general, ellipsis has been considered primarily a semantic phenomenon: what survives ellipsis (in most examples, a noun phrase or prepositional phrase) is taken to be an initial entry in, or a replacement for, some unknown slot in some unknown semantic "chunk" that can be recovered from the immediately preceding discourse. The problem is to identify both that chunk and that slot being filled or replaced. The only use of syntactic structure is to guide this search under the assumption that a surviving constituent, if it is meant to replace something, will have a syntactic form similar to that which it is meant to replace. <*5>

4. The Range of Antecedents and Referents

This section is intended to provide more background on what the text seems to make available to discourse anaphora. As the following pages show, the range is quite broad.

4.1 Individuals

Consider the following sentences.

6. John ate a banana split. Then **he** got sick.

<*5>. I believe this is an accurate, if somewhat simplified characterization of how ellipsis is treated in SOPHIE [Burton, 1976], the SRI speech system [Grosz, 1977], LIFER [Hendrix, 1977] and PLANES [Waltz & Goodman, 1977].

7. Mary gave Sue a T-shirt. It didn't fit.

8. Whether John buys a used car or a new bike, he will keep it in the garage.

9. Blend a cup of flour with some butter. Moisten it with some milk, then knead it into a ball.

10. Mary became a violinist because she thought it a beautiful instrument.

In all cases, the singular definite pronouns - "he", "she" or "it" - refer to a unique individual. However, observe their antecedents closely and consider where they come from. Example 6 is simple: the referent of "he" is something named "John". But in example 7, the referent of "it" is not "a T-shirt", which does not denote a unique individual in the way that "John" presumably does. Rather, the referent of "it" is something that can be described as "the just-mentioned T-shirt that Mary gave Sue". Moreover, in example 8, the referent of "it" is neither "a used car" nor "a new bike", but rather something that can be described as "the used car John buys if he buys a used car or the new bike he buys otherwise". In example 9, the referent of "it" can be described as "the flour-butter mixture gotten by blending a cup of flour with some butter", and in example 10, it is "the violin". This range of individual referents already far exceeds that of the prototypical examples "John" and "Mary" common to many studies of anaphora. However, I have just begun to list the possibilities.

4.2 Sets

Now consider the following sentences.

11. Mary took her kids to DR, where she bought them T-shirts.

12. Few linguists smoke. They know it causes cancer.

13. Mary gave each girl a T-shirt, but none of them fit.

14. Several linguists smoke, although they know it causes cancer.

15. When Mary takes John to the airport, they go by taxi.

In all cases, the referent of the plural definite pronoun "they" is a unique set. But it should be clear that the relationship between referent and text is different in each case. In example 11, the referent of "them" can be described as "Mary's kids" (presuming "her"="Mary"). In example 12, the referent of "they" is the entire set of linguists. (That of "it" is "smoking", cf. Section 4.6.) In example 13, the referent of "them" is not explicit: in fact it can be described as "the set of T-shirts, each of which Mary gave to some girl". In the same vein, the referent of "they" in example 14 is "the set of linguists, each of whom smokes". Finally, in example 15, the referent of "they" is the set comprising "Mary and John".

4.3 Stuff

By "stuff", I mean intuitively continuous things like water, string, silicon, etc. which can be individuated by selecting out a particular quantity, e.g. a cup of water, a piece of string, the silicon in sample 10005. Often stuff can also be individuated in idiosyncratic ways: "a chocolate" has the sense of a bonbon, "a string" has the sense of a piece of string, and "a wine", the sense of a type of wine. "It" can refer to one such individual and "they", to many such. The referent of a singular definite pronoun can be a particular quantity of stuff (however individuated) or the stuff itself as a generic type. For example,

16. John bought beer yesterday, but it seems to be gone.
17. While water covers 75 percent of the earth, it has not been
found on the moon.

In sentence 16, the referent of "it" can be described as "the specific quantity of beer that John bought yesterday", while in sentence 17, the referent of "it" satisfies the description "(generic) water" (not "the water that covers 75 percent of the earth").

4.4 Generics

A plural definite pronoun can also refer to a generic class, as in examples 18 and 19.

18. A Rhodesian ridgeback bit me yesterday. **They** are really vicious
beasts.
19. The Rhodesian ridgeback down the block bit me yesterday. **They**
are really vicious beasts.

In both cases, the referent of "they" is not a particular set, as in the examples of Section 4.2, but rather the generic class of Rhodesian ridgebacks. In both cases, I am making the generic statement that on the whole Rhodesian ridgebacks are vicious. (Notice that such generic class references are possible independent of whether the initial noun phrase is definite or indefinite. It is also independent of whether the initial noun phrase is singular, as in examples 18 and 19, or plural as in example 20.

> 20. While my two Rhodesian ridgebacks are tame, **they** are usually vicious beasts.

In this latter case, it may be unclear whether the plural pronoun refers to the generic class or to the specific set.)

4.5 Prototypes

Another thing that can be referred to with a definite pronoun is a prototypical <x> or something associated with a prototypical <x>. Examples 21-22 illustrate the situation in which this can occur - namely, following an assertion about "each <x>", "every <x>" or "no <x>".

> 21. Every prince, at some point in his life, starts to think about becoming king. **He** begins to plan how to finance his yacht.

> 22. Each man I saw today was carrying a package. I asked **him** if I could open **it**, but **he** refused.

In Example 21, the referent of "he" is the prototypical prince one should have in mind as a result of the first sentence. In Example 22, the referent of "it" is the package being carried by the prototypical man I saw today (the referent of "him" and "he") whom one has in mind after the first sentence of that pair.

4.6 Actions, Events, States, Propositions, ...

Intuitively, since I haven't defined the terms, it is the case that actions, events, propositions, states, types of events, and more can be referred to with the singular definite pronoun "it". For example,

> 23. John dunked Mary's braids in the inkwell.
>   **It** made her cry.

24. John dunked Mary's braids in the inkwell.
    Although **it** usually made her cry, today she held back.

25. John dunked Mary's braids in the inkwell.
    In fact, if anyone does **it**, she will cry.

26. John dunked Mary's braids in the inkwell.
    Then he did **it** to Sally.

27. To prove that all cats have three legs,
    let's assume its converse.

What made Mary cry, i.e. the referent of "it" in example 23, was the
specific event of John's dunking Mary's braids in the inkwell. What
makes her cry, i.e. the referent of "it" in example 24, is **any** event
involving her braids being dunked in the inkwell. This I would consider
a type of event, rather than a specific one. The referent of "it" in
example 25 is the action of dunking **Mary's** braids in the inkwell, while
in example 26, it is that of dunking **someone's** braids there. In example
27, the referent of "it" is the proposition "all cats have three legs".

4.7 Descriptions

Thus far, I have characterized part of the range of referents for
definite pronouns in English. Notice that not only is this range large,
but it is not at all obvious how the text and these referents are
related. This relationship will be a major concern of this thesis.

To continue though, there are other types of anaphoric expressions
in English besides definite pronouns. Consider the following sentences.

28. Mary bought a green tie-dyed T-shirt, and Fred bought a mauve
    one.

29. Mary brought the boys some tie-dyed T-shirts. Fred took the
    mauve **one**.

30. I have a '71 Ch. Figeac and a '75 Durkheimer Feuerberg in the
    cellar. Shall we have the German **one** first?

The antecedent of the anaphoric term "one" in all these cases is a
descriptor, i.e. a way of describing things. In examples 28 and 29, it
is the explicit descriptor "tie-dyed T-shirt", while in example 30, it
is the implicit descriptor "wine" or "bottle of wine".

4.8 Predicates

Earlier I mentioned that an action, like "someone's dunking Mary's braids in the inkwell", could serve as the referent of a definite pronoun. More generally, any predicate contained in the discourse, including ones predicating actions, can be accessed anaphorically. Ways of accessing predicates include verb phrase ellipsis, "do so" anaphora, "gapping" (cf. [Sag, 1976]) and "stripping". So parallel to the examples in Section 4.6, there is

31. First Sam dunked June's braids in the inkwell. Then Max did **0**.

where the antecedent of the ellipsed verb phrase is "dunk Mary's braids in the inkwell". Other examples of predicates as antecedents include

32. Bruce prefers cats as pets, and Wendy **0**, dogs.
    0 = prefer as pets

33. Garth beats his wife. The governor of New Hampshire does **0** too.
    0 = beat Garth's wife, beat his own wife

34. Mary plans to go to Spain and Sue plans to go to Crete, but neither of them will **do so** if their father is ill.
    do so = go to the place she is planning to go to

                    * * * * * * * *

For this thesis, I started out to accomplish two tasks. The first was to identify precisely what the text makes available to three of the aforementioned types of anaphora - definite pronouns, "one"-anaphora and verb phrase ellipsis. I assumed that the range of things that could be accessed in one of these three ways was broad enough that the demands of the other types will not be fundamentally different. My second goal was to develop a set of representational conventions for sentences, as well as procedures for operating on them, which would guarantee for a natural language understanding system that the correct antecedent or referent for an anaphoric expression would always be among the candidates it was able to identify. Although I soon realized that accomplishing these tasks was beyond the scope of one thesis, I believe that the points I make about each type of anaphora (summarized at the end of each chapter), as well as the procedures I develop for identifying their potential antecedents and referents, are a necessary step towards the development of effective machine understanding of anaphoric language.

5. Fundamental Assumptions

In this section, I want to introduce the basic ideas unifying this research. All of them will be expanded upon in later chapters. The first is the notion of a discourse model. My assumption is that one objective of discourse is to communicate a model: the speaker has a model of some situation which, for one reason or another, s/he wishes to communicate to a listener. Thus the ensuing discourse is, at one level, an attempt by the speaker to direct the listener in synthesizing a similar model. (In this sense, I am equating "understanding" with "synthesizing an appropriate model".)

Informally, a discourse model may be described as the set of entities "naturally evoked" by a discourse and linked together by the relations they participate in. These I will call **discourse entities**. (I can see no basic difference between what I am calling "discourse entities" and what Karttunen [1976] has called "discourse referents". My alternate terminology rests on wanting to keep "referent" a separate technical term.) The entities "naturally evoked" by the discourse may have the properties of individuals, sets, stuff, events, activities, etc. (cf. Section 2).

In order to become familiar with the notion of entities "naturally evoked" by a discourse, consider the following sentence.

    35. Each 3rd-grade girl brought a brick to Wendy's house.

Then consider each continuation in example 36. In each case, I would label the referent of the definite pronoun (i.e., "she", "it" or "they") an entity "naturally evoked" by sentence 35.

    36a. **She** certainly was surprised.
        she = Wendy

      b. **They** knew she would be surprised.
        they = the set of 3rd-grade girls

      c. She piled **them** on the front lawn.
        them = the set of bricks, each of which some 3rd-grade girl
        brought to Wendy's house

      d. She was surprised that they knew where it was.
        it = Wendy's house

      e. Needless to say, it surprised her.
        it = the brick-presenting event

Now a speaker is usually not able to communicate at once all the relevant properties and relations s/he may want to ascribe to any one of these discourse entities. That task requires multiple acts of reference. When the speaker wants to refer to an entity in his or her discourse model, s/he may do so with a definite pronoun. In so doing, the speaker assumes (1) that on the basis of the discourse thus far, a **similar** entity will be in the listener's (partially formed) model and (2) that the listener will be able to access and identify that entity via the minimal cues of pronominal reference. The **referent** of a definite pronoun is thus an entity in the speaker's discourse model which s/he presumes to have a counterpart in the listener's discourse model.

Alternatively, the speaker may refer to an entity in his or her discourse model by constructing a **description** of it in terms of some or all of its known properties and/or relations (e.g., "a red balloon", "Mary's mother", etc.). The speaker may or may not assume that the entity has a counterpart in the listener's discourse model. Thus in referring to that entity, the speaker may have one of two intentions: s/he may intend to point the listener to its counterpart in the listener's discourse model or s/he may intend to cause such a counterpart to be **evoked** into the listener's model. In the latter case, such a newly evoked entity would have the properties specified in the speaker's description as well as the property of having been mentioned at that point in the discourse. (Together I will consider these properties to constitute a unique description of the entity which I will call its "invoking description" or **ID**.) The speaker may then felicitously refer to it with a definite anaphor (i.e. a definite pronoun or a definite description).

So while a discourse entity E may be the **referent** of a definite anaphor **A**, I shall consider **A**'s **antecedent** to be **E**'s **ID**, which has been conveyed to the listener by the immediately preceding text. The relationship between the discourse or the spatio-temporal context on the one hand, and the referents of definite pronouns on the other is thus an indirect one, mediated by the discourse participants' models.

As for "one"-anaphora, my assumption is that a "one"-anaphor substitutes for a description. That description is in turn its **antecedent**. There are at least two possible reasons a speaker may have for using a "one"-anaphor in discourse: brevity and contrast. Often these two reasons coincide, brevity enhancing the intended contrast. For example, in preferring large green apples to small **ones**, the use of **ones** both shortens what I need to say and makes the size contrast more evident.

Another set of assumptions I am making concern the ways in which discourse entities can be evoked into the listener's model. These are (1) linguistically, from the explicit discourse; (2) perceptually, from the immediate spatio-temporal environment; and (3) inferentially, reasoning from the existence of other discourse entities. (Perceptual evocation of discourse entities is another way of looking at the "pragmatically controlled" definite pronouns discussed in Hankamer & Sag [1976].)

These three are also factors in what descriptions become associated with entities in the listener's discourse model. First, the discourse itself provides explicit descriptions. These may reflect things like the speaker's knowledge and attitudes (e.g. "a rock" as opposed to "a fine-grained porphyry"), the speaker's beliefs about the listener's knowledge, the speaker's intentions (e.g. a desire to indicate an inherent relationship between a predicate and its argument

    38a. The man who invented the mini-skirt deserves the rack.
      b. A prominent French couturier deserves the rack.)

Perception is a second factor in what descriptions the speaker and listener become aware of. As mentioned above, an entity may be evoked into the speaker or listener's discourse model as a result of what s/he **perceives**. How it is **described** will depend upon how s/he classifies that perception linguistically. As well as it can be presented on paper, the following is an example of a "one"-anaphor substituting for the speaker's description of some sense perception.

    39. [Bonnie goes up to a balloon man at the circus and says]
        "Do you have a blue **one** with green stripes."
        one = balloon

Finally, inference is a third factor in what descriptions a discourse participant assigns to entities in his or her discourse model. Among other things, the speaker assumes the listener can and will follow the speaker's unspoken lead to infer:

1. from description d_1 of some entity in his or her discourse model, another description d_2 of that same entity;

2. from entities $e_1,...,e_j$ with descriptions $d_1,...,d_j$ respectively, a new discourse entity e_k with description d_k.

For instance, in sentence 40 the speaker assumes that the listener both can and will infer from the description "Ch. Figeac '71" another description for that same entity - namely "wine". Similarly for the descriptions "'76 Fleurie", "Ockfener Bockstein '75" and "Durkheimer Feuerberg '75". The "one"-anaphor then substitutes for the non-explicit shared description "wine".

40. I have a '71 Ch. Figeac, a '76 Fleurie, a '71 Ockfener Bockstein and a '75 Durkheimer Feuerberg in the cellar. Shall we have the German **ones** for dinner tonight.
    ones = wines

It should be clear, even from this brief summary of my fundamental assumptions, that descriptions are critical to this approach to discourse anaphora. (Discourse entities are basically no more than hooks for descriptions.) One fundamental task I have posed for myself then is to identify those aspects of the text which are essential to forming appropriate descriptions (**IDs**) of the discourse entities evoked by the text.

It will turn out that significant aspects of the text can be specified in terms of the **structure** of a suitable representation. In fact, this will be a major sub-theme of this thesis: resurrecting structure from its too often down-played role in mature language understanding. <*6> In the next chapters, I will propose as a suitable representation, a pair consisting of a sentence's surface syntactic parse tree and a type of logical interpretation which will be introduced in Chapter 2, Section 3. I will show that both of these play a role in

<*6>. I recognize that children may have a completely different mode of language understanding, that for them meaning may be the key to structure, rather than the other way around (cf. Macnamara [1972]).

discourse understanding (viewed here as model synthesis). Moreover, since the listener can be presumed to be both aware of and focused on the most recent set of representations s/he has constructed, the speaker can take advantage of them via anaphoric expressions to reduce the amount of material s/he must make explicit. This goes not only for definite and "one" anaphora, but for verb phrase ellipsis as well. (As I will show in Chapter 4, any of the surfacy logical interpretations that one may assign to a sentence can provide the trigger for a subsequent instance of verb phrase ellipsis.)

Before I close this section, I want to mention one more assumption which is also a caveat. I am assuming that an English definite pronoun (e.g. "he", "hers", "it", "them", etc.) can fill two different roles in a sentence. It can function as the natural language equivalent of a bound variable in logic, indicating that several argument places in a formula are to be filled equivalently [Partee, 1972] or it can be used to refer to a discourse entity, following the discussion earlier in the section.

Often these two roles coincide, with no immediate semantic difference arising from which one is attributed to the given pronoun. For example, in the sentence

41. Garth beats his wife.

the role of "his" may be to show that a single object fills both the subject of "beat" and the "possessor" of "wife". That is, Garth is the person who beats his own wife. On the other hand, "his" may function to refer to the discourse entity describable as "the person named Garth". In that case, Garth is the person who beats Garth's wife. Locally the effect of both roles is the same. However if sentence 41 were to be followed by a sentence like

42. Fred does 0 too.

the effect of the two roles would be different. In the first (bound variable) case, this sentence would be interpretable as "Fred also beats his own wife", and in the second, as "Fred also beats Garth's wife". While this particular situation will be discussed further in Chapter 4, Section 2.2, the point to be aware of is the dual role of definite pronouns and the ambiguity this may introduce. (A similar point is made in [Sag, 1976].)

6. Thesis Organization

This thesis has a very simple organization. In Chapter 2 I will consider the representational and procedural demands of handling definite pronoun reference to individuals and sets. I will present a formalism for representing a type of logical interpretation of a sentence and show how a simple rule for forming IDs can be articulated with respect to the **structure** of such interpretations. I will also illustrate the process of synthesizing a discourse model from a text and show how it complements the process of resolving definite anaphora. In Chapter 3 I will consider the representational and procedural demands of handling "one" anaphora and in Chapter 4, I will do the same for verb phrase ellipsis. Chapter 5 presents a summary of the research reported here, as well as some initial remarks on three interesting problem areas into which it might be extended: (1) the relationship between data-driven and expectation-driven processes in model synthesis; (2) reference-handling in limited contexts and (3) anaphoric reference to discourse entities evoked by sentences and larger units of text.

TABLE OF CONTENTS

CHAPTER 2. Definite Pronouns

1. Introduction

1.1 The Notion of a Discourse Model

To set the context for this chapter on definite pronoun anaphora, I want to review and expand upon some remarks I made in Chapter 1 concerning the notion of a discourse model. I said there that I am assuming that one objective of discourse is to communicate a model. The speaker has a model of some situation which s/he wishes to communicate to a listener. The ensuing discourse is, on one level, an attempt by the speaker to direct the listener in synthesizing a similar model.

Essential to my view of a discourse model is that it contains a collection of entities, recording their properties and the relations they participate in. <*1> A speaker is usually not able to communicate at once all the relevant properties and relations associated with one of these **discourse entities**. That task requires multiple acts of reference. When the speaker wants to refer to an entity in his or her discourse model, one way s/he may do so is by using a definite pronoun. In so doing, the speaker assumes (1) that on the basis of the discourse thus far, a **similar** entity will be in the listener's (partially formed) model and (2) that the listener will be able to access and identify that entity via the minimal cues of pronominal reference. <*2> The **referent** of a definite pronoun is thus an entity in the speaker's discourse model, which s/he presumes to have a counterpart in the listener's discourse model. Discourse entities may have the properties of individuals, sets, events, actions, states, facts, beliefs, hypotheses,

---

<*1>. [Collins, Brown & Larkin, 1977] contains an interesting discussion of other aspects of discourse models and their role in story understanding.
<*2>. While I am claiming that anything that can be referenced pronominally is a discourse entity, I am not claiming that every discourse entity can be referenced pronominally. This will be an important point later when I argue that it is not only for pronoun reference that one needs to form appropriate descriptions for discourse entities evoked by the text.

properties, generic classes, typical set members, stuff, specific quantities of stuff, etc. (See Chapter 1, Section 2.)

An alternative way the speaker has of referring to an entity in his or her discourse model is to construct a **description** of it in terms of some its properties (e.g. "a red balloon", "the refrigerator in Wendy's kitchen", etc.). In doing so, the speaker may or may not be assuming that the entity has a counterpart in the listener's discourse model. Thus the speaker may have one of two intentions. If s/he assumes a counterpart in the listener's discourse model, the intention may be to point the listener to it. If s/he doesn't assume a counterpart, the intention may be to **evoke** one. If all goes right in the latter case, the newly evoked discourse entity will have the properties specified in the speaker's description as well as the property of having been mentioned at that point in the discourse. (Together I will consider these properties to make up a unique description of the entity which I will call its "invoking (or introductory) description" or its **ID.**) The speaker may then felicitously refer to that entity with a definite anaphor (i.e. a definite pronoun or a definite description), reasonably confident of the listener's ability to identify its referent.

So while a discourse entity **E** may be the **referent** of a definite anaphor **A**, I shall consider **A**'s **antecedent** to be **E**'s ID - that is, the unique description of **E** conveyed to the listener by the immediately preceding text. The relationship between the discourse or external situation, on the one hand, and the referents of definite anaphora, on the other, is thus an indirect one, mediated by the discourse participants' models. <*3>

<*3>. There are other views about antecedents and referents as well. One restricts the term "referent" to things in the real world. Thus in a discourse about future or hypothetical worlds, some definite pronouns will have antecedents but no referents, e.g.

    (i) a. Bruce hopes to catch a fish.
       b. He wants to eat it for dinner.

Here the pronoun "it" has an antecedent - presumably something like "the fish Bruce catches if his hope to catch a fish materializes" - but **no** referent, unless the sentence is taken to imply that the speaker has some particular real world fish in mind.

Note that a discourse model is not meant to be equivalent to a person's complete memory (knowledge base). I am taking it as a formal structure which at any point in the discourse validates the sequence of propositions communicated up to that point. It is irrelevant whether those propositions are in accord with a person's previous knowledge or whether the discourse or elements of it will be remembered. This conception of a discourse model also implies that it is not equivalent to "consciousness" or "focus", as these terms have recently been construed, although it is related [Chafe 1974, 1976; Grosz 1977]. That is, according to Chafe only those items presumed to be in the listener's consciousness can be referred to pronominally or with decreased stress. This seems to circumscribe some part of what the speaker would presume to be in the listener's discourse model. Grosz's use of "focus" also overlaps the sense in which I am using "discourse model". She views the "focus" of the discourse at point p as containing those items relevant to the interpretation of the current utterance either because they have participated explicitly in the discourse prior to p or because they are closely related to another item that has.

1.2 The Importance of Descriptions

Now no actual discourse is ever sufficient to fully determine a model - an infinite number of models can satisfy any given discourse. Thus the listener has the option, in a sense, to determine it further. The specific discourse model synthesized by a listener in response to any given discourse may have **additional** characteristics which are derived from his or her memory (prior knowledge). In particular, a discourse entity may possess characteristicss **other than** those provided explicitly in the discourse because:

But **if** one adopts this viewpoint, I am certain that one also has to invent a new term to refer to non-real world "constructs" that the listener may be learning more and more about as the discourse proceeds. Moreover, since I believe that there is no type of anaphora which picks out possible world "constructs" and not real world "referents" (or vice versa), nothing is gained by distinguishing for the purposes of anaphora those entities which have a real world counterpart from those which don't (and only labelling the former "referents"). However, it is obviously necessary to include in one's description of an entity its

1. The listener's knowledge base contains information of a **universal** sort about holders of a given property or fillers of a given role in a given situation. So for example, if the listener learns in the discourse that "Mary had a little lamb", and s/he knows all lambs have the property of being either white or black, then s/he knows of Mary's just-mentioned little lamb that it is either white or black. (Whether listeners actually **access** their memory to flesh out their discourse models is another story. In fact, this is one of the difficult problems being explored in Artificial Intelligence of "When to stop inferencing? When to start?")

2. The listener's knowledge base contains information of a **particular** sort about an entity which satisfies the properties and relations given explicitly in the discourse. For example, the listener "knows" Mary: s/he heard about her last week or s/he knows Mary from bridge club, etc. As a result, new properties (and perhaps new entities as well) may be added to the still under-determined discourse model in connection with the discourse entity e_1 with the directly given property "firstname = Mary". Moreover, the listener's memory may also contain an entity which may be described in the same way as discourse entity e_2 - "little lamb which e_1 has". As a result, the former entity's further properties and relations may be brought in and associated with e_2, which constrains the listener's discourse model even more. It is no longer just "the recently mentioned little lamb ...", it is Snookums.

The point of all this **vis a vis** anaphora is that it leads me to distinguish two kinds of descriptions: **invoking** descriptions (**IDs**) <*4> - ones formed solely from information conveyed by the explicit discourse - and **prior** descriptions - ones formed from information drawn from the listener's knowledge base. (Of course, for a description to be prior does not imply that a person **knows** its possessor in any way other than linguistically. The entity and the information about it may simply exist in the person's memory as a result of an earlier discourse.) Descriptions are vital in so far as they direct the ways that people can reason about the things they describe. One place such reasoning is required is in anaphor resolution. That is, in order to decide which of

---

existential status, such information being needed by those inference procedures which are to decide among candidate antecedents.
<*4>. In [Nash-Webber & Reiter, 1977] these were called "intensional descriptions". However I have become wary of using the term "intensional" since it is being used in so many different ways by so many different people. Under the circumstances, "invoking (or introductory) description" seems a better choice.

the discourse entities e_1 and e_2 the "it" of "its fleece was white as snow" refers to, it is necessary to know how e_1 and e_2 can be described.

Now there are circumstances in which prior descriptions are not forthcoming. They are either impossible or impractical for the listener to derive from his or her knowledge base: **impossible** because there are no entities there that satisfy the given description or because no particular entity is implied (e.g. "Bruce wants to marry a lawyer, but he doesn't care how brief **she** is."); **impractical** because for example, several otherwise different entities may satisfy the given description (e.g. "Bruce brought a chair in to be re-covered". Bruce has several chairs. Which one did he bring in?) Deriving additional information about the referent of an anaphoric term (e.g. "it" or "the chair") would then depend on choosing between these different entities. (If it's his armchair, then it once belonged to his mother. If it's a dining room chair, then it has a mahogany veneer.) That in turn, may either be expensive or impossible. To cope with such circumstances requires the ability to reason about an entity in terms of its "invoking description" (**ID**), e.g. "the just-mentioned chair that Bruce brought in to be re-upholstered") and thus the ability to derive an appropriate **ID** in the first place.

Towards this end, I will discuss in detail some important formal aspects of noun phrases that must be taken into account in deriving appropriate **IDs** for the discourse entities evoked by a text - i.e., aspects which can be articulated in terms of the **structure** of some suitable sentence-level representation. <*5> I shall then show how to use such a representation for recognizing the entities evoked by a text and deriving their **IDs**. Of course, other aspects of sentences besides the ones I have discussed in detail must be taken into account as well in forming appropriate **IDs**, e.g. tense, modality, negation, disjunction, etc. Some of these are discussed briefly in Section 5.

<*5>. While I will only be talking here about descriptions of individuals and sets, I believe that these remarks have relevance to deriving descriptions of other things like events and quantities of stuff as well. See the discussion under "Future Research" in Chapter 5, Section 2.

1.3 Warnings to the Reader

There are three important points that the reader must have clear if this chapter is to be effective. First, the reader must be aware that English is frequently ambiguous with respect to **just those aspects** of a sentence which are critical to forming appropriate discourse entity IDs. I am not just talking about analyzing sentences out of context, a known way of introducing false ambiguities: it must be acknowledged that even the previous context may not be sufficient to lead the listener to correct quantifier scope assignments or to identify the intended scope of negation. However in many cases, a definite anaphor may enable the listener to simultaneously (1) disambiguate the intended sense of a previous sentence; (2) form appropriate **IDs** for the entities thereby evoked; and (3) resolve the anaphoric term against its intended referent. What enables the listener to do all this is the fact that alternative possible interpretations do not lead to equally satisfying ways of resolving the anaphor. This is something that ought to be kept in mind in the design of natural language understanding systems: that resolving anaphora may lead to understanding, as well as the other way around.

The second point that must be clear is that the properties of a discourse entity present in the speaker's model cannot always be determined unambiguously from the noun phrase **initially** used to describe and reference it. If the listener makes a wrong assumption in incrementing his or her discourse model in response to that noun phrase, the new discourse entity will have different properties than its counterpart in the speaker's model. As a result, subsequent attempts by the speaker to refer to this discourse entity anaphorically may fail, since its properties differ from those of its counterpart in the listener's discourse model.

The following example will illustrate the problem. Consider the noun phrase "five dollars". In using this phrase, the speaker may be referring to either (1) an individual - a quantity of money worth five dollars - or (2) a set - for example, five one dollar bills. Now consider the following sentence

1. Bruce gave Wendy five dollars.

If the phrase "five dollars" causes a discourse entity with only set-type properties to be evoked in the listener's model, the listener may be at a loss to identify the individual referent of "it" in the sentence

2. **It** was more than he gave Sue.

On the other hand, if discourse entity with only individual-type properties is evoked, the listener may be at a loss to identify the set referent of "them" in a subsequent sentence like

3. One of **them** was counterfeit.

This has clear implications for machine-based understanding, as I shall discuss later in Section 2.5.

The third important point is that a single noun phrase may evoke several discourse entities in the listener's model which are not alternative perspectives in the sense of example 1 above. The reader may recall my noting in Chapter 1, Section 4.4 that both definite and indefinite noun phrases can evoke a discourse entity corresponding to a generic class. This will be **in addition to** the specific individual or set that it evokes, and **both** entities will be available to pronominal reference. <*6>   For example,

    4a. The Great Dane down the block treed a VW yesterday.
      b. Then **it** ate the VW, wheels and all.
      c. **They** are really large dogs.
        it = the Great Dane down the block
        they = the generic class of Great Danes

1.4   Chapter Organization

The top-level organization of this chapter is as follows: in the next four sections (Sections 2-5), I shall discuss some issues involved in **synthesizing a discourse model**, with a machine-based understanding system playing the part of the listener. In discussing these, my aim is to motivate some procedures which must be carried out in order to form

---

<*6>. How to treat the evocation of generic discourse entities in a way that is both effective vis a vis anaphor resolution and efficient computationally is an interesting problem that will probably not have a good answer until the proposals made here for synthesizing a discourse model have been integrated into a working system.

appropriate IDs for the discourse entities evoked by a text (Section 2).
I shall then show how English noun phrases can be represented in a
formal way which captures structurally what is needed in part for
forming discourse entity IDs (Section 3). I shall present a preliminary
rule for doing this - an ID-rule - which is sensitive to
quantificational aspects of noun phrases (Section 4). For a more
sophisticated ID-rule, other aspects of sentences must be taken into
account as well. These I discuss briefly in Section 5. Finally in
Section 6, I shall outline the process of synthesizing a discourse model
from a text and argue for its feasibility. In so doing, I shall show
how it is complementary to the more usually discussed process of anaphor
resolution.

2. Factors in Forming Discourse Entity IDs

As I mentioned in the last section, it is necessary to take account
of a variety of sentential features in order to form appropriate IDs for
the discourse entities evoked or referenced in a text. I have
specifically identified the following eight, which I shall discuss at
greater length in Sections 2.1-2.6 below:

(1) It is necessary to distinguish between definite and indefinite
    noun phrases. This is true whether the noun phrase is
    singular or plural. For each non-standard determiner
    ("several", "many", "few", etc.), it is both necessary and
    sufficient to identify whether it acts like a definite or
    indefinite determiner vis a vis ID formation.

(2) Any ellipsed verb phrases in the sentence must be resolved
    before appropriate IDs can be formed.

(3) For each modifier in a plural noun phrase, it is necessary to
    distinguish whether it conveys information about the entire
    set denoted by the plural noun phrase or about the individual
    set **members**. (This may not be determinable when the sentence
    is first received.)

(4) For a sentence containing one or more indefinite plural noun
    phrases, it is necessary to recognize what the sentence is
    predicating of each set so denoted and/or what it is
    predicating of each individual set member. (This too may not
    be determinable when the sentence is first received.)

(5) It is necessary to identify the speaker-intended quantifier
    scope assignments, although they may not be determinable when
    the sentence is first received.

(6) If there are any definite pronouns in the sentence, it is necessary to determine whether they could be interpreted intra-sententially as bound variables. This can be important in so far as quantifier scope assignments are concerned, but again may not be determinable at the time the sentence is first received.

(7) It is necessary to realize that certain noun phrases, specifically those determined by "each", "every" or "no" are ambiguous vis a vis whether the speaker is referring to a set-like discourse entity or a prototype discourse entity (9cf. Chapter 1, Section 4.5).

(8) It is necessary to distinguish whether a noun phrase occurs in a relative clause or in the matrix sentence, as it can affect both intra-sentential pronoun resolution and the formulation of appropriate discourse-dependent descriptions.

(As I shall not be proposing a specific formalism until Section 3, these discussions will be somewhat informal. Moreover, I am also aware of other features which must be considered in forming appropriate IDs for the entities evoked by the discourse. Although I have not explored them in the same detail, I shall discuss several of them briefly in Section 5.)

2.1 Noun Phrase Specificity

2.1.1 The Definite/Indefinite Distinction

The point I want to argue here may be an obvious one: that definite and indefinite noun phrases must be represented in distinct ways. The specific reason for arguing this derives from the fact that the referent of a definite pronoun must satisfy a unique description of which both speaker and listener are aware. While both definite and indefinite noun phrases in the same context can evoke discourse entities, the operation that constructs the description of such entities is very different for the two cases. <*7> Looking first at singular noun phrases, compare the following sentence pairs.

<*7>. As I mentioned in Section 1.1, definite descriptions can be used in two ways: they can be used like definite pronouns to refer to entities presumed to be in the listener's discourse model or they can be used to evoke new entities into that model. It is the latter use of definite descriptions that is relevant here.

5a. Wendy bought the yellow T-shirt that Bruce had admired.
 b. It cost twenty dollars.

6a. Wendy bought a yellow T-shirt that Bruce had admired.
 b. It cost twenty dollars.

In either case, the referent of "it" has a unique description of which both discourse participants are aware. In the first case, it is the **explicit** description "**the** yellow T-shirt that Bruce had admired". (This description is the antecedent of "it".) In the second case, it is the derived description "the yellow T-shirt that Bruce had admired, that Wendy bought, **and** that was mentioned in sentence 6a." To see that only this description can be presumed by the participants to describe the referent of "it" uniquely, notice that sentence 6a. can be uttered truthfully if Bruce had admired several yellow T-shirts or even if Wendy had bought several such T-shirts. Thus it does not even presuppose that there is a unique yellow T-shirt that Bruce had admired and that Wendy bought. But it does **mention** only **one** such T-shirt. As such, the above description picks out one entity uniquely, and that is the referent of "it".

The point is that the entity evoked by a singular definite noun phrase can be described uniquely by just that description. The entity evoked by a singular indefinite noun phrase can only be described uniquely via a conjunction of (1) the description inherent in the noun phrase (e.g. "yellow T-shirt that Bruce had admired"); (2) a predicate that embodies the remainder of the sentence (e.g. "which Wendy bought"); and (3) a predicate that relates that entity to the sentence evoking it (e.g. "which was mentioned in (or evoked by) sentence 6a."). This is the description which I have labelled the entity's "invoking description" or **ID**. <*8>

Notice that in order to form the second of these predicates, any ellipsed verb phrases in the sentence must first be resolved. If left unresolved, a sentence like

---

<*8>. While I have been talking in terms of **the** entity evoked by a noun phrase, the reader should keep in mind that both definite and indefinite noun phrases also evoke generic-type discourse entities as well (cf. Section 1.3; also Chapter 1, Section 4.4).

7. A woman whom Wendy knows is too.

would evoked a discourse entity which could only be described as "the just-mentioned woman whom Wendy knows who is too". While this may be a unique description, it is not very useful from the point of view of reasoning about the entity so described (cf. Section 1.2).

Another reason why ellipsed verb phrases must be resolved is that the antecedent of an ellipsed verb phrase may itself contain indefinite noun phrases. If left unresolved, discourse entities will fail to appear and subsequent definite anaphors, fail to have referents. This problem of "missing antecedents" [Grinder & Postal, 1971] is discussed further in Chapter 4, Section 4.

The same characteristic behavior of definites and indefinites just discussed for singular noun phrases holds for plural noun phrases as well. The referent of the definite plural pronoun "they", like the referent of a definite singular pronoun, must satisfy a unique description known to both speaker and listener. While both indefinite and definite plural noun phrases in context may evoke uniquely describable set entities, the procedure for forming their descriptions differs in the two cases. Consider the following example.

8a. I saw **the** guys from "Earth Wind & Fire" on TV today.
  b. I saw **the three** guys from "Earth Wind & Fire" on TV today.
  c. I saw **all three** guys from "Earth Wind & Fire" on TV today.
  d. I saw **some** guys from "Earth Wind & Fire" on TV today.
  e. I saw **three** guys from "Earth Wind & Fire" on TV today.

9. **They** were being interviewed by Dick Cavett.

Sentence 8a-c each contain a definite plural noun phrase. Corresponding to that noun phrase, a discourse entity will be evoked into the listener's discourse model which can be uniquely described as "the (set of) guys from 'Earth Wind & Fire'". This can be verified by following either of these sentences by sentence 9 and considering what is the referent of the definite pronoun "they". <*9>

<*9>. While sentences 8b&c. provide the additional information that the number of guys in "Earth Wind & Fire" is three [not actually true - BNW], that information is not needed in order to describe the set uniquely. However, it should not be discarded as it may be needed later in resolving a definite anaphor like "the three guys".

Sentences 8d&e, on the other hand, each contain an **indefinite** plural noun phrase. The discourse entity that each of these noun phrases in context ·evokes can only be described uniquely as "the (set of) guys from 'Earth Wind and Fire' that I saw on TV today **and** that was mentioned in Sentence 8d(e)." This is because either sentence is consistent with there being other members of "Earth Wind & Fire" whom I didn't see on TV today, as well as other members whom I did see but whom I don't mean to include in my statement. <*10> Notice again that the set size information provided in sentence 8e. is not necessary for describing that set uniquely. However, it too may be useful later in resolving definite anaphora.

2.1.2 The Referential/Attributive Distinction

Having argued that procedures for deriving appropriate discourse entity IDs must distinguish between definite and indefinite noun phrases, I shall now argue why it is not necessary **for this purpose** to distinguish between what linguists and philosophers have called "attributive" and "referential" uses of definite noun phrases [Donnellan, 1966] or between "specific" and "non-specific" uses of indefinite ones [Fillmore, 1967]. That is, I shall argue that one definite operator and one existential operator will suffice for representing sentences at a level suitable for modeling definite anaphoric reference. <*11>

<*10>. This latter point is a subtle one, and usage may vary from person to person. That is, some people intend an indefinite plural noun phrase contained in a sentence S - "Some <x>s P" - to refer to the **maximal** set - i.e., "the set of <x>s which P". Other people· intend it to refer to some subset of that set - "the set of <x>s which P which I (the speaker) intended to mention in sentence S". For a system to cope with this variation in usage, it would be better for procedures to derive the latter, non-maximal set description, which is always appropriate. If a system is sophisticated enough to associate a "belief space" with the speaker, other procedures can later access that belief space (if necessary or desirable) to judge whether the maximal set interpretation might have been intended. (This will again become an issue when I discuss other determiners like "many" and "several" later on in this section.)   .
<*11>. Not all linguists and philosophers see these as real ambiguities. Kaplan [1968-69], for example, sees them as extremes on a continuum of "vividness", where vividness is a measure of how much the

Partee [1972] uses the following sentence to illustrate the difference between an "attributive" and a "referential" use of a definite noun phrase.

10. The man who murdered Smith is insane.

This can be understood as either the speaker's asserting of the particular individual referred to by the definite noun phrase that that individual is insane (i.e. the "referential" use) or his asserting that whatever individual it is who satisfies the presumed unique description "man who murdered Smith", that that individual is insane (i.e. the "attributive" use).

Looking at this from the point of view of the speaker's discourse model, in the former case the speaker presumes to have some tie between a discourse entity describable as "the man who murdered Smith" and some specific individual "out there". In the latter case, s/he doesn't. Essentially the former reduces to the speaker's having other descriptions for this entity which don't follow from **general** axioms based on the given description "the man who murdered Smith". (e.g. Every person who murders someone is a murderer. Therefore the man who murdered Smith is a murderer.) Nevertheless in either case, s/he **still** has one and only one such discourse entity in his or her model, and that is all that matters for definite pronoun reference. A definite pronoun refers to a unique discourse entity, independent of how many descriptions it satisfies: just as long as the given one is enough to make it unique. Notice that if sentence 10 were followed by a sentence like

11. **He** ought to be locked up.

the antecedent of "he" would still be the unique description "the man who murdered Smith", whether the speaker knows anything more about that individual or not. (While I shall not do so here, a similar argument can be constructed for definite plural noun phrases, based on examples like

---

speaker knows about an individual. Essentially I agree with this. However as I shall mention again later, I feel that the issue of how much the listener presumes the speaker knows about any individual is a matter of pragmatic and not semantic concern.

12. The men who murdered Smith are insane.
    They ought to be locked up.)

Thus I do not feel it necessary to distinguish between "attributive" and "referential" definite noun phrases in order to derive appropriate **IDs** for discourse entities and, consequently, possible antecedents for definite pronouns. <#12>

2.1.3 The Specific/Non-specific Distinction

As to the specific/non-specific distinction for indefinite noun phrases, a similar argument to the one above holds here as well. <#13> For example, consider

13. Bruce plans to marry a woman his parents disapprove of.

The speaker is held to be using the noun phrase specifically if s/he has a specific individual "out there" in mind who s/he describes as "a woman Bruce's parents disapprove of", i.e.

> Bruce plans to marry Farah Fawcett-Majors, a woman his parents disapprove of.

Moreover, the speaker makes no assumption that "woman whom Bruce's parents disapprove of" describes any individual uniquely, hence the speaker's use of the indefinite rather than the definite determiner. On the other hand, an indefinite noun phrase is assumed to be used non-specifically if the speaker is just relating someone's plans, desires, thoughts, etc. Within those plans in this case, is an individual with the property of being a woman Bruce's parents disapprove of. Neither existence nor uniqueness "out there" is presumed in any way.

However in the speaker's discourse model, the description "the hypothetical individual asserted to be in Bruce's planning space who is

---

<#12>. On the other hand, it may be important for the listener to ascertain what else, if anything, the speaker presumes to know about that individual in order to better model the speaker's beliefs. That is, the significance of these distinctions is pragmatic rather than semantic.
<#13>. Partee [1972] argues that these are not two different distinctions at all, that the referential/attributive "ambiguity" can be extended to cover indefinites as well, doing away with a distinction between specific and non-specific indefinites.

a woman, whom Bruce parents disapprove of, whom he plans to marry, and who was mentioned in sentence 13" is satisfied by only one discourse entity. It is irrelevant at this point whether that entity corresponds to someone who exists "out there" or not. Solely by virtue of its unique description, it can be referred to with a definite pronoun, e.g.

    14. He will elope with **her** to Uruguay.

Thus it does not appear important to identify how an indefinite noun phrase is being used in order to form an adequate description of the discourse entity it evokes. <*14>

    (A similar argument can be constructed for an indefinite plural noun phrases, as in example 15.

    15. Bruce plans to ride on some llamas when he is in Peru.
        He hopes that **they** won't protest too much.

Here the speaker uses "they" to refer to the discourse entity uniquely describable as the set of llamas asserted to be in Bruce's planning space, which he plans to ride on when he is in Peru, and which was mentioned in sentence 15". Whether "some llamas" is being used specifically or non-specifically - i.e., whether the speaker has some particular llamas in mind when s/he utters sentence 15 - does not appear significant for constructing an appropriate description of the discourse entity that has been evoked.)

2.1.4 Non-standard Determiners

    Up to now, I have only illustrated my arguments about noun phrase specificity with relatively standard (logically speaking) definite determiners - "the", "the six" "all the", etc. - and relatively standard indefinite ones - "a", "some", "six", etc. However, English has other determiners which may be in even more common use - "many", "several", "few", "almost all", etc. I shall now show that these determiners divide themselves into two classes, depending on whether they act like definite or indefinite determiners vis a vis evoking discourse entities.

<*14>. Again this is not to say that this distinction is irrelevant in general: it may be very important for the listener to know what the speaker presumes to know about Bruce and his plans in order to better model the speaker. That is, the significance of the distinction is again pragmatic rather than semantic.

One consequence of this is that the ID-rule to be given in Section 4 does not have to treat these determiners as special cases.

To see the difference between these determiners, consider the following pairs of sentences.

16a. Few linguists smoke since **they** know it causes cancer.
  b. Many linguists smoke although **they** know it causes cancer.

17a. Few linguists compute though **they** know it can be useful.
  b. Many linguists compute since **they** know it can be useful.

In both "few" sentences (16a & 17a), the referent of "they" is the discourse entity uniquely describable as "(the entire set of) linguists". That is, "few <x>s" evokes the same discourse entity as the definite noun phrase "the <x>s". <*15> The "many" sentences (16b & 17b) are different. There the pronoun "they" can be interpreted as referring to the entity uniquely describable as "the just-mentioned set of linguists who smoke (compute)". That is, the sentence "Many <x>s P" can be seen to evoke a discourse entity which is similar to that evoked by the sentence "Some <x>s P". The difference is the additional information that can be associated with the "many" discourse entity that the just-mentioned set of <x>s which P is large or larger than the speaker feels the listener might expect. <*16> (As I mentioned earlier, both "many <x>s" and "few <x>s" can evoke a discourse entity corresponding to the generic class of <x>s as well. However, the referent of "they" in the "few" sentences above does not appear to be ambiguous, perhaps because the distinction between the set of <x>s and the generic class of <x>s is a subtle one.

One might observe in passing that the reverse polarity determiner "not many" acts like "few" vis a vis evoking discourse entities, i.e., the opposite of "many". For example,

18. Not many linguists smoke since **they** know it causes cancer.
    they = (the entire set of) linguists

<*15>. Although the sentences assert that the subset of linguists who smoke (compute) is small in the speaker's opinion, that subset does **not** appear to be available to pronominal reference. What concerns me here is that the entire set is.

<*16>. I am not concerned here with what semantics a system should assign to these non-standard determiners, except insofar as it affects the discourse entities they take part in evoking.

19. Not many linguists compute although **they** know it can be useful.
    they = (the entire set of) linguists

However, a NEG which occurs in the sentence auxiliary does not effect this same change in behavior (cf. example 20)

20. Many linguists don't smoke since they know it causes cancer.
    they = the just-mentioned linguists who don't smoke

Of the "non-standard" determiners, I believe that "not many", "not all" and "almost all" can be treated like "few" vis a vis evoking discourse entities, and that "most", "several" and "(quite) a few" can be treated like "many" in this regard. (Recall that the point I wanted to make was that there are no other ways determiners will act, so that a rule for forming discourse entity IDs need not treat these as special cases.

The following examples provide some evidence to back up the above classification. (For the determiners which act like indefinite plurals, the reader should keep in mind that a generic-type discourse entity may also be evoked, so there may be two possible referents for the subsequent anaphor.)

21. Not many linguists drive Porsches: **they** prefer to eat.
    they = the linguists, *the linguists who drive Porsches,
           *the linguists who don't drive Porsches

22. Though not all linguists like Gin, **they** won't refuse it.
    they = the linguists, *the linguists who like Gin,
           *the linguists who don't like Gin

23. Almost all linguists like Scotch. **They** also like Vodka.
    they = the linguists, *the linguists who like Scotch,
           *the linguists who don't like Scotch

24. Most linguists attended the masquerade. **They** each came as a different transderivational constraint.
    they = the linguists who attended the masquerade

25. Several linguists attended the masquerade. **They** dressed up as cyclic transformations.
    they = the linguists who attended the masquerade

26. (Quite) a few linguists attended the masquerade. **They** all came as parse trees.
    they = the linguists who attended the masquerade.

2.2 Member/Set Information

One important observation about plural noun phrases which is relevant to anaphora and the formulation of appropriate IDs is that the noun phrases themselves contain descriptive information about sets as well as about their constituent members. For example,

27a. three dotted lines which intersect at point P
   b. the three dotted lines which intersect at point P

"Dotted" is a property of each individual line. "Three", on the other hand, supplies information about the **cardinality** of those sets of lines which satisfy these descriptions. Moreover, the relative clause - "which intersect at point P" - does not directly restrict which **individual** lines belong to these sets, but rather specifies a property of appropriate **sets** of three lines. Prenominal, prepositional and clausal modifiers within a noun phrase may all be used to describe either a set as a unit or the set's individual members.

One place where handling anaphora demands that a distinction be drawn between set information and member information within a plural noun phrase is in describing the entity evoked by an embedded noun phrase. Consider the following pairs of sentences

28a. Three men who tried to lift a piano dropped **it**.
   b. The three men who tried to lift a piano dropped **it**.

29a. Three men who tried to lift a piano dropped **them**.
   b. The three men who tried to lift a piano dropped **them**.

If the relative clause is meant to restrict particular **sets** of three men, as in example 28, then "it" can refer to the discourse entity describable as "the just-mentioned piano which the just-mentioned three men tried to lift". However, if the relative clause is meant to restrict each particular man under discussion, as in example 29, then "they" can refer to the entity describable as "the just-mentioned pianos, each of which one of the just-mentioned men tried to lift". (This is an example where a subsequent sentence disambiguates an earlier one.)

2.3 Three Uses of Plurals

As I mentioned earlier, when a sentence contains one or more plural noun phrases, one must distinguish what the sentence is predicating of each set so denoted and what it is predicating of each individual set member. That is, I see distributive quantification <*17> as only one of three distinct senses that a sentence containing a plural noun phrase can be used to convey. The three senses I call **distributive**, **conjunctive** and **collective**. Consider for example

30. Three boys bought five roses.

This can be used to convey either:

a. that Boy1 bought five roses, Boy2 bought five roses and Boy3 bought five roses (**distributive**); or

b. that the total of rose-buying boys is three and the total number of roses, each of which was bought by some rose-buying boy, is five (**conjunctive**); or

c. that three boys (formed into a consortium) bought five roses (**collective**).

It is important for the listener to understand which sense is intended by the speaker because each has different implications. For example,

a. If sentence 30 is understood distributively, then it implies that each of the boys **owns** five roses as a result of the transaction.

b. If it is understood conjunctively, then it implies (at least in my idiolect) that each of the boys owns at least one (or part of one) rose as a result.

c. If it is understood collectively, then it does not imply that any individual boy owns any roses as a result of the transaction. Only the consortium is implied to own roses as a result, and it owns five.

The fact that these senses have different implications means, in turn, that it may be important for anaphora that the listener distinguish among them. One reason can be seen by comparing the following sentences.

<*17>. I shall often refer to universal quantification by the more expressive phrase "distributive quantification". This carries for me the flavor of distributing something similarly over each member of a set.

31a. The three boys ordered a large anchovy pizza.
   b. Because of the heavy traffic, **it** was delivered cold.

32a. The three boys each ordered a large anchovy pizza.
   b. Because of the heavy traffic, **they** were delivered cold.

(Placing "each" after the subject in sentence 32a. makes its distributive intent explicit.) <*18> Because English has a different pronoun for referring to a set than to an individual, the distributive use of a plural must be distinguished from a conjunctive or a collective use. <*19> Only when a plural is used to convey distributive quantification can it change the discourse entity evoked by a singular noun phrase within its scope from an individual to a set. This means that a different pronoun would be used to refer to it.

Specifically, in sentence 31b., the discourse entity that "it" refers to is the **individual** describable as "the large anchovy pizza mentioned in sentence 31a, which the three boys ordered." In sentence 32b., the discourse entity that "they" refers to is the **set** evoked by the **same** noun phrase, this time describable as "the set of large anchovy pizzas, each of which was ordered by one of the three boys, which was mentioned in sentence 32a."

A more general reason why it may be important to distinguish which plural sense was intended is that the **ID** of the discourse entity evoked by an embedded existential will be different in each case. This in turn may be significant in anaphor resolution: depending on its **ID**, the discourse entity may be more or less appropriate as the referent of a definite anaphor. Consider again example 30.

<*18>. An "each" or "every" noun phrase (e.g. "each boy", "every gnu") has only a distributive sense. An "all" noun phrase, on the other hand, may be used to convey either a distributive or a collective sense. For example,
   (i) All the policemen in this town are fat. (distributive)
   (ii) All the policemen in this town got together to save my cat.
        (collective)
Notice the strangeness of example (iii), whose verb phrase demands a collective reading, where its subject is "each policeman", which has only a distributive sense.
   (iii) ?Each policeman in this town got together to save my cat.
<*19>. Or conversely, as I mentioned in Section 1, a subsequent instance of pronominal reference may be sufficient grounds for choosing a particular unambiguous sense for the sentence.

30. Three boys bought five roses.

Depending on which sense of "three boys" the speaker means to convey, the description appropriate to the discourse entity evoked by "five roses" will be something like

a. "the set of roses, each of which belongs to a set of five roses which one of these three rose-buying boys bought and was mentioned in sentence 30" (distributive)

b. "the set of five roses, each of which one of the three rose-buying boys bought (in part or in **toto**)" (conjunctive)

c. "the set of five roses which this rose-buying consortium of three boys bought" (collective)

2.4 Pronouns in the Input

If one steps back for a moment, one may recall that my reason for synthesizing a discourse model is to make sure that appropriate discourse entities are around when definite anaphora are being resolved. However, a sentence about to be examined for the discourse entities it evokes or refers to may itself contain definite pronouns. As I shall show below, these must be resolved (or at least certain candidates ruled out) before appropriate discourse entity IDs can be formed.

To be more concrete (although still somewhat informal), consider the following sentence.

33. Someone was using each telephone on **his** desk.

Depending on how the quantifiers are scoped, sentence 33 may be paraphrased in one of two ways.

(i) For each telephone on **his** desk, there was someone who was using that telephone.

(ii) There was someone who was using each telephone on **his** desk.

If one assumes that "his" in sentence 33 is coreferential with "someone", then only paraphrase (ii) is possible. On the other hand, if one assumes that "his" refers to some previously mentioned discourse entity, then either paraphrase is possible.

But notice the difference in discourse entities evoked by the universally quantified noun phrase in each paraphrase. In the case of (i), it evokes a discourse entity describable as "the (set of) people, each of whom was using some telephone on the desk of that previously mentioned man". (cf. "John had to make a call. He was understandably upset then, when he saw that someone was using each telephone on his desk. His response was to call **them** all ninnies.") In the case of paraphrase (ii), the corresponding discourse entity can be uniquely described as "the just-mentioned person who was using each telephone on his (own) desk". (cf. "Someone was using each telephone on his desk. **He** was trying unsuccessfully to make a conference call.")

Recall that my point is that pronouns present in an input sentence must be resolved (or at least certain possibilities ruled out) before appropriate **IDs** can be formed for the discourse entities it evokes. In the case of sentence 33, if neither pronoun nor quantifiers are resolved, it is unclear which of the following three very different IDs is right for the newly evoked discourse entity.

(a) the (set of) people, each of whom was using some telephone on the desk of that previously mentioned (but not yet identifiable) man

(b) the just-mentioned person who was using each telephone on the desk of that man

(c) the just-mentioned person who was using each telephone on his (own) desk.

However, if all possibilities can be ruled out except someone/"his" coreference (the "bound variable" interpretation, cf. Chapter 1, Section 5), then quantifier scope must be as in paraphrase (ii), and (c) is the appropriate **ID**. On the other hand, if the "bound variable" possibility can be ruled out, then it **only** depends on being able to identify the speaker-intended scope assignment in order to decide whether (a) or (b) is correct. However, it will never depend on which of the remaining possibilities "his" is resolved against. Thus although some decision must be made about each definite pronoun in the sentence, they do not need to be completely resolved in order for an appropriate (if somewhat vague) **ID** to be formed. (I will mention this point again in Section 6, where I discuss discourse model synthesis and anaphor resolution.)

2.5 Alternative Perspectives

In Section 1.3, I mentioned that it was not always possible to determine certain properties of a discourse entity in the speaker's model, given the noun phrase initially used to describe and reference it. The example I gave to illustrate this required the listener to have the world knowledge that the phrase "five dollars" could refer **inter alia** to either a single quantity of money worth five dollars or a set of one dollar bills. The individual/set distinction involved here is an essential one as far as anaphora is concerned because of the separate ways that individuals and sets are referred to with definite pronouns. (I shall use the word **status** for the property of discourse entities whose possible values include individual, set, stuff, event, etc.)

Another case where a discourse entity's status cannot be identified immediately is where a noun phrase is determined by "each", "every" or "no". In that case, the speaker may have in mind either the set of <x>s (communicating something about each individual member) **or** the prototypical <x> (communicating something in terms of that individual, cf. Chapter 1, Section 4.5). While these perspectives may be interchangeable truth-functionally, they are different with respect to reference: in the first situation, the speaker can later refer to this discourse entity as "they" and in the second, as "he", "she" or "it" (depending on what is appropriate).

To see this consider the following examples.

34. (Every, each) man in the park today was carrying a snowball. **He** was trying to hold it discreetly, but it kept dripping.
    he = the prototypical man in the park today
    it = the just-mentioned snowball that the prototypical man in the park today was carrying

35. (Every, each) man in the park today was carrying a snowball. **They** gave the **snowballs** to Wendy, who threw **them** at Fred.
    they = the set of men in the park today
    them, the snowballs = the set of snowballs, each of which some man in the park today was carrying

36. No intelligent woman likes Nixon. **She** would be crazy to.
    she = the prototypical intelligent woman

37. No intelligent woman likes Nixon. **They** all think him a traitor.
    they = the set of intelligent women

Notice in the first two examples that when the listener's perspective is the prototype (example 34), the **ID** of the entity evoked by the indefinite noun phrase "a snowball" is appropriately phrased in terms of this prototype - "the just-mentioned snowball which the prototypical man in the park today was carrying". On the other hand, if the speaker focuses on the set of men (example 35), the **ID** of this entity is "the set of snowballs, each of which some man in the park today was carrying". It is extremely important to keep track of these dependencies if anaphoric terms are to be resolved correctly.

There are two other points here which are important computationally. First, one may not be able to tell **ab initio** what the speaker's perspective is, given the evidence of an "each", "every" or "no" noun phrase. To deal with this, one may want to cause a discourse entity to be evoked into the system's discourse model (i.e. the system as listener) which could be viewed in either way until some subsequent anaphor in the input forced a choice. Secondly, there are only minor differences between an **ID** phrased in terms of a prototype and one phrased in terms of a set. This can be seen by aligning the above IDs:

(i) the prototypical man in the park today
    the entire set of men in the park today

(ii) the just-mentioned snowball which the prototypical man in the
     park today was carrying
     the set of snowballs, each of which some man in the park today
     was carrying

That is, in processing "each", "every" or "no" noun phrases, the semantic core of the **ID** could be formed immediately. The prototype or set specifications could then be attached, if and when the speaker "reveals" his or her viewpoint. This is the tack I will be taking in Section 4.

2.6 Embedded Noun Phrases

I mentioned at the start of this section that it was important to distinguish whether a noun phrase occurred in a relative clause or in the matrix sentence. I said that it was important both for resolving intra-sentential pronominalization and for forming appropriate discourse entity **IDs**. In this section I will first discuss relative clause noun

phrases vis a vis intra-sentential pronominalization and then in terms
of discourse entities.

To begin, consider the role of "it" in each of the following
sentences. <*20>

    38a. Every man who owns a donkey beats it.
      b. A man I know who owns a donkey beats it.
      c. The man who·owns a donkey beats it.
      d. Which man who owns a donkey beats it.
      e. No man who owns a donkey beats it.

Intuitively, "it" is related to the embedded noun phrase "a donkey".
Since the referent of a definite pronoun must satisfy a unique
description of which both speaker and listener are aware (cf.
Section 2.1.1), one might describe the referent of "it" as "the donkey
he owns", where "he" stands for the bound variable associated with
"(each, a, the, which, no) man who owns a donkey" (cf. Chapter 1,
Section 5). In so doing, one is essentially viewing this referent as a
"local discourse entity" internal to the sentence, a "parameterized
individual" (i.e., parameterized by the bound variable) to use a term
borrowed from [Woods & Brachman 1978]. <*21>

The "parameterized individuals" internal to the above sentences are
different from the "actual" discourse entities the sentences evoke.
Specifically, they all have the **same ID**, independent of how the noun
phrase containing the relative clause is determined. On the other hand,
the actual discourse entities that can be referred to anaphorically in
subsequent sentences do not.

To illustrate this disparate behavior, consider the following
examples.

    40a. Every man who owns a donkey beats it.
        it = the donkey he owns
      b. However, **the donkeys** are planning to get back at **them.**

<*20>. The problem posed by these sentences and others like them has
been discussed often in the linguistics and philosophy literatures (cf.
[Bartsch 1976; Hintikka & Carlson 1977; Edmondson 1976]).
<*21>. The phrase "parameterized individual" is being used somewhat
loosely to include "parameterized" sets, stuff, etc., cf.

    39. No man who owns two donkeys beats them.
       them = the two donkeys he owns

the donkeys = the set of donkeys, each of which some man who
                owns a donkey owns
them = the set of men, each of whom owns a donkey

41a. A man I know who owns a donkey beats it.
     it = the donkey he owns
  b.*But **the donkeys** are planning to get back at **him**.
     the donkeys = ???
  c. But **the donkey** is planning to get back at **him**.
     the donkey = the just-mentioned donkey that the just-mentioned
                  man who owns a donkey and beats it owns
     him = the just-mentioned man who owns a donkey and beats it

42a. The man I know who owns a donkey beats it.
     it = the donkey he owns
  b.*But **the donkeys** are planning to get back at **him**.
     the donkeys = ???
  c. But **the donkey** is planning to get back at **him**.
     the donkey = the just-mentioned donkey that the man I know
                  who owns a donkey owns
     him = the man I know who owns a donkey

43a. Which man who owns a donkey beats it?
     it = the donkey he owns
     -- "None"
  b.*But **the donkeys** are planning to get back at {**him**, **them**, ???}.
     the donkeys = ???
  c.*But **the donkey** is planning to get back at {**him**, **them**, ???}.
     the donkey = ???

These examples show that while the "parameterized individuals" local to
the (a) sentences have the same local **ID** and can be referenced in the
same way **intra-sententially**, the **ID** of the actual discourse entities
evoked depends on how the matrix noun phrase is determined.

In Section 4.3.3, I shall show formally how to construct "local"
IDs for the parameterized individuals evoked by embedded noun phrases,
as well as regular **IDs** for the actual discourse entities they evoke.

3. Representational Conventions

In Section 2, I discussed several features of a sentence which must
be taken into account in forming appropriate discourse entity **IDs**. If
ID formation is to be carried out automatically, as it must in
man/machine communication, sentences must be represented in such a way
that these features stand out clearly. In this section, conventions are
suggested for such a representation adequate for **ID** formation (what I
will call a **Level-2** semantic representation). First however, I will set

this representation in context by outlining the process of **ID** formation as I see it. (This is a highly abbreviated version of the discussions in Section 6 and in Chapter 4, Section 4. Among other things, I will ignore most of the contingencies required for dealing with ambiguity.)

As each sentence comes into the system, I assume it will be parsed into a surface syntactic parse tree following some simple conventions of $\overline{X}$ syntax [Jackendoff, 1977]. Then rather than trying to produce a Level-2 representation directly from the parse tree, <*22> I will assume that it is first interpreted into a intermediate semantic representation - what I shall call a **Level-1** representation - which reflects only such semantic material as can be derived from either the parse tree or semantic information present in the lexicon. (This would include characterizations of each verb in terms of n-place predicates (what Bresnan [1978] calls its "logical argument structure"), semantic selectional restrictions on what can fill each argument place, the relationship of a verb's syntactic structure to its logical structure - i.e., the mapping from syntactic roles to argument places, etc.)

Then I assume that the Level-1 representation will be converted into a Level-2 semantic representation via a process of resolving ellipsed verb phrases, quantifier scope ambiguities and definite pronouns (or at least identifying whether a bound variable, or parameterized entity interpretation is possible); identifying whether

---

<*22>. Recall from Section 2 that a representation adequate for **ID** formation must indicate **explicitly**:
    a. the number and specificity of each noun phrase, and whether it occurs in a main or relative clause
    b. the verb phrase of each clause (i.e., ellipsed verb phrases must be resolved)
    c. the correct placement of each noun phrase modifier; for plural noun phrases, an indication as to whether the modifier conveys properties of the set or its members
    d. the correct scope of each quantifier
    e. either the referent of each definite pronoun or whether it can function as a bound variable, parameterized entity or discourse anaphor (with specific referent unknown)
    f. whether a sentence containing a plural noun phrase is predicating something of the set or of its individual members
Recall also from Section 2 that it is possible that many of these cannot be determined immediately.

or not a definite noun phrase is anaphoric and if so, replacing it with
the label of its referent, etc. (For a sentence with several clauses, I
assume that the conversion process will apply to each clause, starting
from the leftmost, most embedded one.) Finally, I assume that
ID-formation will involve applying the ID-rule to be presented in
Section 4 to the leftmost quantifier or definite description in the
Level-2 interpretation, identifying the discourse entity it evokes,
forming a new representation in terms of that entity and then repeating
the procedure for the next term (cf. Section 6). (These latter
interpretations I will call "referential forms" of the Level-2
interpretation. They will also play a role in resolving ellipsed verb
phrases, cf. Chapter 4, Section 2.3.)

The representational conventions proposed here are adequate to
convey the distinctions required of a Level-2 representation.   However,
since it is often possible to make these distinctions early on, in
converting from a parse tree into a Level-1 semantic interpretation,
these conventions are appropriate for a Level-1 representation as well.
The difference is that among the terminal symbols of the Level-1
representation will be additional ones to indicate unresolved pronouns
and ellipsed verb phrases (e.g. HE, IT, THEY, P?, etc.).   Among the
additional terminal symbols of the Level-2 representation will be
discourse entity names (e.g. e_1, e_2, etc.). <#23> (For directions in
which these representations might be further extended, see Section 5.)

3.1 Noun Phrases in General

The assumption that both quantifier scope and verb logical argument
structures are explicit in a Level-2 representation (and can be explicit
in a Level-1 semantic representation as well) implies a logical
formalism. However, a "flat" predicate calculus formalism will not
suffice, as it does not facilitate a structural distinction between a
predicate associated with a sentential verb phrase and a predicate

---

<#23>. Both Level-1 and Level-2 representations should be viewed as
conceptual formalisms in that they allow things to be stated clearly on
paper. However they would not necessarily be implemented in this way.

associated with another part of the sentence. <*24>   For example,

44. Some cotton T-shirts are expensive.
    (Ex) . Cotton x & T-shirt x & Expensive x

Without this distinction, it becomes impossible to resolve ellipsed verb
phrases (cf. Chapter 4), a necessary step in producing a Level-2
representation.   Moreover, there is no way in a "flat" predicate
calculus representation to distinguish a noun phrase in a relative
clause from one in a matrix clause. As I argued in Section 2.6, this is
also necessary for an adequate treatment of anaphora.

   The   convention   I   suggest   is   an   extension   of   **restricted
quantification.** In restricted quantification, a quantification operator
(e.g. ∀,E), the variable of quantification and the class it ranges over
(noted   implicitly   as   a   predicate)   constitute a structural unit of the
representation - i.e., (Qx:P) where Q is a quantification operator, x
the variable of quantification and P, a predicate. (I will call this
unit a **quantifier** and the class, a quantifier class restriction, or
Q-restriction.   For example, "Every boy is happy" can be represented as

    (∀x:Boy) . Happy x

This is truth functionally equivalent to

    (∀x) . Boy x ==> Happy x

Similarly "Some boy is happy" can be represented as

    (Ex:Boy) . Happy x

which is truth functionally equivalent to

    (Ex) . Boy x & Happy x

   To extend this notation to include relative clauses is quite
simple.   Semantically, a relative clause can be viewed as a predicate,
albeit a complex one.   One way to provide for arbitrarily complex
predicates is through the use of the abstraction operator, represented
as " λ " by [Hughes & Cresswell, 1968] (following [Church, 1941]) and
" ∧ " by [Montague, 1974].   I will adopt the former convention.   For
example, the noun phrase "a peanut" can be represented as

    (Ex:Peanut)

___

<*24>. An adequate treatment of indefinite plurals will be presented in
Section 3.3.

while the noun phrase "a peanut that Wendy gave to a gorilla" can be
represented as

   (Ex: λ(u:Peanut)[(Ey:Gorilla) . Gave Wendy,u,y])

This follows the same format (Qx:P) as above. In this case

      λ(u:Peanut)[(Ey:Gorilla) . Gave Wendy,u,y]

names a unary predicate which is true if its argument is a peanut that
Wendy gave to some gorilla. The predicate associated with the head noun
("peanut") is indicated in a structurally distinct way (i.e., in the
position usually associated with a variable type) for reasons associated
with resolving "one"-anaphora (cf. Chapter 3, Section 3.2).

3.2 Singular Noun Phrases

   I argued in Section 2.1 that in order to form appropriate discourse
entity IDs, it was necessary to indicate whether a noun phrase was
singular or plural, definite or indefinite. I shall use the definite
operator (i) for singular definite noun phrases, representing them as
definite descriptions of the form

      i<variable>:<S>

where S is an open sentence free in <variable>. For example,

      ix:T-shirt x   "the T-shirt"
      ix:λ(u:T-shirt)[Bought Sue,u] x   "the T-shirt Sue bought"
      ix:λ(u:T-shirt)[Yellow u] x   "the yellow T-shirt"

In the Level-1 representation, definites being used anaphorically will
not (since they cannot) be distinguished from ones being used to evoke
new discourse entities in the listener's discourse model. I assume this
will be done in converting into a Level-2 semantic representation, as
part of a single procedure for handling definite descriptions.

   Singular definite noun phrases could instead have been represented
by introducing a new quantification operator, say THE or E!, for "there
exists a unique". While it doesn't affect what can be represented, the
choice of approach will slightly affect the specification of an ID-rule
or procedures for deriving possible antecedents for ellipsed verb
phrases or "one"-anaphora. The reason is that a quantifier <*25> like

_____

<*25>. Recall that I am using the term quantifier to refer to the
triplet of (1) quantification operator (∀ or E), (2) variable of

(E!x:T-shirt) or (THE x:T-shirt) scopes an open sentence, while a term formed with the definite operator merely fills an argument place to a predicate. Rather than introducing a new quantifier, I shall use the definite operator to form terms.

Indefinite singular noun phrases will be distinguished from definite ones by representing them using standard existential quantification, e.g.

> (Ex:T-shirt)   "a T-shirt"
> (Ex:λ(u:T-shirt)[Bought Wendy,u])   "a T-shirt Wendy bought"
> (Ex:λ(u:T-shirt)[Yellow u])   "a yellow T-shirt"

They could as well have been represented as terms, using the indefinite operator $\in$ in the format $\in$<variable>:<S>, where <S> is an open sentence in <variable>, for example $\in$x:T-shirt x - "a T-shirt". But again, the only difference for deriving antecedents would come from the fact that the quantifier term would scope an open sentence while the indefinite term would, like a constant, only fill an argument place to a predicate.

3.3 Plural Noun Phrases

The standard logical way to specify a set is via its defining properties - i.e., {u|Pu} represents the set of things u for which Pu is true. P may be any arbitrary predicate, simple or complex. <*26>   For example,

> {u|Man u}
> "the set of men"
>
> {u|λ(v:Man)[Fat v]u}
> "the set of fat men"

---

quantification and (3) the class being quantified over. The result of adopting this notation is frequently a 1:1 mapping between English noun phrases and quantifiers in the formal representation. The exceptions include predicate nominative noun phrases which interpret as predicates rather than quantifiers (cf. Chapter 3, Section 3.2) and plural noun phrases, which in some cases must be interpreted as a sequence of two quantifiers. The latter case is discussed later in Section 3.3.
<*26>. A set may also be specified **explicitly** via a list of its members, i.e. $\{t_1,\ldots,t_n\}$, where t_i is either a constant term (terminal or functional) or an indefinite description, e.g. {Carol, husband-of(Carol), ix:λ(u:Man)[Love Carol, u]}, the set consisting of Carol, Carol's husband and the man Carol loves.

{u|λ(v:Man)[(Ex:Piano) . L v, x]u}
"the set comprising each man who lifted a piano"
(Here L stands for "lifted".)

However, this notation is inadequate to represent all plural noun phrases for the purpose of forming appropriate IDs, as it does not allow one to predicate things about the sets themselves. This is because {u|Pu} always refers to the **maximal** set of u's such that Pu is true. For example, this notation is inadequate to represent noun phrases like

45. three men who tried to lift a piano
46. massed bagpipe bands

The sense of example 45 is **some** set of men, of cardinality three, who together tried to lift a piano.

One way to remedy this deficiency is to introduce a way of getting at the subsets of a given set. The standard mathematical notion of a power set provides one notation for this. The power set of a given set is the complete set of its subsets. The mathematical notation used to indicate the power set of the set A is 2^A. This reflects the fact that the size of the power set of a set is 2 raised to the size of the set. Corresponding to this, but in terms of predicates (whose extensions are sets) rather than in terms of sets directly, I will introduce a function, **set**, which takes predicates on individual x's to predicates on sets of x's. For example, if Man is a predicate which is true if its argument is an individual man, then **set**(Man) is a predicate which is true if its argument is a **set** of men. Similarly, if

λ(v:Man)[(Ey:Piano) . L v,y]

is a predicate true if its argument is an individual who lifted a piano, then

λ(v:**set**(Man))[(Ey:Piano) . L v,y]

is a predicate true if its argument is a set of men such that the set of them lifted a piano. On the other hand,

set(λ(v:Man)[(Ey:Piano) . L v,y])

is a predicate which is true if its argument is a set of men such that **each** of them lifted a piano.

At this point I should also like to introduce another function - **maxset** - which serves essentially the same purpose as the implicit set notation - {u|Pu} - given above. Like **set**, **maxset** takes a predicate **P** on x's to a predicate on sets of x's. However **maxset(P)** will be true of its argument only if that argument is the maximal set of x's for which **P** is true. That is

   maxset(P)c   iff   c = {u|Pu}

My reason for introducing **maxset** is a cosmetic one: that is, it allows all definite plural noun phrases to be represented as definite descriptions with the iota operator.

Now adopting these **set** and **maxset** functions permits both definite and indefinite plural noun phrases to be represented correctly. <*27> Indefinite plurals can be represented just like indefinite singulars using the existential operator and an appropriate predicate for the quantifier restriction. For example,

   (i) $(Ex:\lambda(v:\textbf{set}(Man)))[(Ey:Piano) . L v,y])$
       "some men who (together) lifted a piano"

   (ii) $(Ex: \textbf{set}(\lambda(v:Man)[(Ey:Piano) . L v,y]))$
        or
        $(Ex:\lambda(v:\textbf{set}(Man))[(\forall u \epsilon v)(Ey:Piano) . L u,y])$
        "some men who (each) lifted a piano"

Definite plurals can be represented like definite singulars using the definite operator and either the **set** or **maxset** function.

   (iii) $ix:\lambda(v:\textbf{set}(Man))[(Ey:Piano) . L v,y]x$
         "the men who (together) lifted a piano"

   (iv) $ix: \textbf{maxset}(\lambda(v:Man)[(Ey:Piano) . L v,y])x$
        "the men who (each) lifted a piano"

In (iv) the definiteness of the plural is captured by the fact that the maximal set of individuals satisfying any given predicate is always unique. <*28> To represent the same sense using the definite operator and the **set** operator is much less efficient, i.e.,

---

<*27>. As I mentioned, one may not be able to determine **ab initio** what "correct" is - in this case, whether noun phrase modifiers apply to the set as a whole or to its individual members. I am assuming that this ambiguity will be reflected in a sentence having several possible Level-1 representations or a single non-committal one if such a representation can be devised.
<*28>. This may of course be maximal only with respect to the given context.

$$ix:set(\lambda(v:Man)[(Ey:Piano) . L v,y])x$$
$$\& (\forall z:set(\lambda(v:Man)[(Ey:Piano) . L v,y])) . z \subseteq x$$

Now, in choosing how and where to represent the remaining information that may be in a plural noun phrase - i.e., set cardinality - it might be useful to indicate it so as to be ignorable when identifying candidate antecedents for "one"-anaphora. <#29> The antecedent of "one" never includes cardinality information unless a phrase like "a set of" appears explicitly in the language. For example, in sentence 47

47. I saw three grubby little boys in the playground and another **one** in the park.

the description "set of three grubby little boys" is not a possible antecedent for "one". (i.e., The second conjunct of sentence 47 cannot be interpreted as "and another set of three grubby little boys in the park".) However it is a possible antecedent in example 48

48. I saw a group of three grubby little boys in the playground and another **one** in the park.

Although there are obviously several ways of augmenting the above representation for plural noun phrases (i-iv) to reflect explicitly given set cardinality, the one that I like is the following. (C here stands for "celebrated" and L, for "lifted".) In parallel with (i)-(iv) above, I would have

(a) $(Ex:\lambda(v:set(Man))[(Ey:Piano) . L v,y]) . C x \& |x|=3$
    "Three men who (together) lifted a piano celebrated."

(b) $(Ex: set(\lambda(v:Man)[(Ey:Piano) . L v,y]) . C x \& |x|=3$
    "Three men who (each) lifted a piano celebrated."

(c) $C ix:\lambda(v:set(Man))[(Ey:Piano) . L v,y]x \& |x|=3$
    "The three men who (together) lifted a piano celebrated."

(d) $C ix: maxset(\lambda(v:Man)[(Ey:Piano) . L v,y])x \& |x|=3$
    "The three men who (each) lifted a piano celebrated."

Notice that the only difference between "some x's" (i-ii) and "n x's" (a-b) is the single extra cardinality term. Since it is only the

---

<#29>. Obviously this only applies if the same representation is to be used as input both to procedures for deriving appropriate discourse entity IDs and for identifying antecedents for "one"-anaphora. If one chooses to use syntactic parse trees as one's hunting ground for the latter, this would not be a forcing function on one's representation.

definite/indefinite information that is critical to correct **ID** formation (and **not** cardinality), this is what is constant in these representations.

   At this point, the reader might be puzzled about the absence of ∀'s, given that in elementary logic, the standard practice is to represent plural noun phrases in terms of universal quantifiers. The standard example of this is

> All men are mortal
> (∀x) . Man x ==> Mortal x

However, this assumes that things are only attributable to individuals, and as I showed in Sections 2.2-2.3, English allows things to be attributed to sets as well. Adopting the above conventions permits a separation of the notions of focussing the listener on a set of things and of saying something about that set or about its individual members. To attribute some property to each member of some set, I would merely add in a universal quantifier <*30> cf.

   49. Three men ate a pizza.
       (Ex:**set**(Man))(Ey:Pizza) . Ate x,y & |x|=3

   50. Three men each ate a pizza.
       (Ex:**set**(Man))(∀w∈x)(Ey:Pizza) . Ate w,y & |x|=3

   51. The three men ate a pizza.
       (Ey:Pizza) . Ate ix:**maxset**(Man)x & |x|=3, y

   52. The three men each ate a pizza.
       (∀w∈ix:**maxset**(Man)x & |x|=3)(Ey:Pizza) . Ate w,y

This was what my earlier remark pertained to when, discussing the mapping between English noun phrases and quantifiers, I said that some plural noun phrases mapped onto a sequence of two quantifiers rather than a single one. <*31>

<*30>. The representation given here differs somewhat from the one I suggest in Chapter 4, Section 2.5 for sentences containing "each" as an adverb. The reason for the different forms is that it is simpler to state the ID-rule in Section 4 in terms of this representation, while it is simpler to state procedures for identifying possible verb phrase antecedents in terms of the other form. However, the forms are easily interconvertable.

<*31>. English also permits distributive quantification over sets of things, as in "Each three men ate a pizza." Unfortunately, this usually means less than it logically could - that is, it is not usually used to imply that any given man participated in more than one trio of

4. Preliminary Rule for Deriving Discourse Entity IDs

As I said earlier, an understanding system must be able to ascribe appropriate **IDs** to the entities evoked in a discourse. As with a human listener, these **IDs** may be what allows the system to reason about the entities and to recognize anaphoric references to them later on. This section then proposes a rule (an **ID-rule**) that a system could use in deriving appropriate **IDs** for the discourse entities evoked by a text. Note that the rule described here should be taken as suggestive rather than definitive. On the one hand, I cannot prove that the **IDs** it produces are correct (although they intuitively seem so), and on the other hand, it does not take into account all the aspects of a sentence that I realize can affect **ID** formation. (In Section 5, I discuss some of these other aspects and their contribution to a more sophisticated rule.)

In the first part of this section, I shall illustrate the ID-rule with some simple examples. Then I shall proceed through its different cases. First I shall show how it derives appropriate **IDs** for the discourse entities evoked by independent quantifiers or definite descriptions (i.e., ones not bound within the scope of another quantifier). Then I shall show how it applies in dependent cases: (1) to existentials within the scope of distributive (universal) quantifiers; (2) to quantifiers and definite descriptions whose class restrictions contain variables bound by other quantifiers and (3) to quantifiers and definite descriptions contained in a quantifier class restriction (i.e., ones corresponding to a noun phrase in a relative clause).

The reader should take note of the following points. First, these cases will probably not be simple to digest. While I was hoping to find a single principle that would account for every discourse entity **ID** associated with any quantifier or definite description in any context,

---

pizza-eaters. Thus a simple representation like

$(\forall x : \lambda(u:\textbf{set}(Man))[|u|=3])(Ey:Pizza)$. Ate x,y

would convey more than was intended. I do not have a better proposal in mind, which would still keep very close to the surface syntax.

no such thing happened. The six cases presented here behave essentially differently.

Secondly, the **IDs** this rule produces are not necessarily the only ones such a rule could derive. That is, a discourse entity may be uniquely describable in several ways, all of which could be derived from form of the original sentence. For example, given the sentence

53. Each girl ate two peaches.

there is a discourse entity evoked which could be uniquely described as either "the set of peaches, each of which belongs to a set of two peaches which some girl ate" or as "the set of pairs of peaches, each of which some girl ate". While this ID-rule only produces the second of these, one description can be converted into the other by purely syntactic means.

Thirdly, as I mentioned earlier, one may not be able to assign a sentence immediately the single Level-2 representation that correct **ID** formation requires. However, in attempting to resolve a subsequent definite anaphor, the rule can be applied to each alternative Level-2 representation of a sentence (or perhaps to a heuristically constrained set of them) to show the consequences in terms of discourse entities (and hence possible referents) of each particular alternative.

4.1 Informal Examples

As a first example, consider the sentence

54. Wendy bought a crayon.

As I mentioned in Section 3, an attempt is made, in converting from a Level-1 into a Level-2 representation, to identify whether a definite description is anaphoric. If so, the label of its referent will appear in the Level-2 representation; if not, it will remain for subsequent processing by the ID-rule. Suppose the definite description "Wendy" is not anaphoric. Then the Level-2 representation of sentence 54 will be

[54-i] (Ex:C) . Bought Wendy,x

(where C stands for "crayon").

Starting from the leftmost term of [54-i], the ID-rule will identify the first discourse entity evoked, say e_1, as "the crayon

mentioned in sentence 54 that Wendy bought" (cf. Section 2.1). This can
be represented as

   [54-ii] ix: C x & Bought e_1,x & **evoke** S_{54},x

Notice that the first term of [54-ii] corresponds to the Q-restriction
in [54-i] and the second term, to its main predication. The third term
uses a predicate **evoke** to relate the discourse entity to the context in
which it was evoked. <*32> To label this point, I use the clause
number, assuming that clauses are numbered in temporal sequence through
the discourse. (A simple sentence such as 54 is a single clause.)
Notice that the third term corresponds to an explicit deictic way of
referring to things in English -- "You know that crayon I **just told you
about**? Well, Wendy's dog ate it."

   After identifying the first discourse entity e_1, a new
interpretation is formed in terms of it - i.e.,

        Bought Wendy, e_1

and the ID-rule is re-applied. This time, the discourse entity evoked,
say e_2, will be identified as "the person named Wendy". e_1's ID can
then be updated to indicate that "Wendy" refers to e_2.

   Notice that if sentence 54 had contained an indefinite noun phrase
instead of "Wendy" - i.e.,

   55. A woman I know bought a crayon.

there would be two semantically equivalent ways of writing its Level-2
interpretation - i.e.,

        (a) (Ex:W)(Ey:C) . Bought x,y
        (b) (Ey:C)(Ex:W) . Bought x,y

(W stands for the complex predicate "woman I know".) This might appear
to lead to a problem since the ID-rule is applied to the leftmost term
first. That is, in (a) the first discourse entity to be evoked, say e_1,
would be identified as

   ix: W x & (Ey:C) . Bought x,y & **evoke** S_{55},x

(a) would then be re-written in terms of e_1 - i.e.,

        (Ey:C) . Bought e_1,y

<*32>. "Context" is a vague term. What I am trying to get at is the
discourse entity's link to and uniqueness within the speaker's
presentation of a situation or topic.

and the ID-rule re-applied to identify the second discourse entity, say
e_2, as

iy: C y & Bought e_1,y & **evoke** S_{55},y

i.e., "the just-mentioned crayon which e_1 bought".

Starting from (b), the first discourse entity, e_1, would be
identified as

iy: C y & (Ex:**W**) . Bought x,y & **evoke** S_{55},y

i.e., "the just-mentioned crayon which a woman I know bought" and the
second, e_2, as

ix: **W** x & Bought x,e_1 & **evoke** S_{55},x

i.e., "the just-mentioned woman I know who bought e_1". In both cases,
the second discourse entity is described in terms of the first, but not
vice versa. If however earlier IDs are updated following the
identification of each subsequent discourse entity, then the fact that
alternative quantifier orders are possible does not lead to different
results.

As a second example, consider the sentence

56. Wendy gave each girl Bruce knows a crayon.

"Wendy" now refers anaphorically to the discourse entity e_2. Assume
that "each girl Bruce knows" is not found to be anaphoric. Then the
Level-2 representation of sentence 56. is

[56-i] $(\forall x:G)(Ey:C)$. Gave e_2,x,y

(where C stands for "crayon" and **G** stands for "girl Bruce knows".)
Viewed from a set perspective (cf. Section 2.5), the first discourse
entity, say e_3, evoked by sentence 56. will be identified as "the set of
girls Bruce knows".

[56-ii] ix:**maxset(G)**x

[56-i] will then be re-written in terms of e_3

$(\forall x \epsilon e_3)(Ey:C)$. Gave e_2,x,y

and the ID-rule will be applied to the existential term. This time, the
discourse entity evoked, say e_4, will be identified as "the set of
crayons, each of which is associated with sentence 56 such that Wendy
gave it to one of those girls".

[56-iii] iz: **maxset**$(\lambda(u:C)[(Ex\epsilon e_3)$. Gave e_2,x,u & **evoke** $S_{56},u])z$

The relationship between [56-i] and [56-ii] shows that given an independent universal quantifier, the ID-rule can identify its associated discourse entity solely in terms of its Q-restriction. As for [56-iii], the **ID** of the existentially evoked entity, notice that within the **maxset** operator, one term comes from the existential's Q-restriction, one term from the main predication, and one term from the label on its evoking clause. This shows that given an existential occurring within the scope of one or more universals, the ID-rule will identify its associated **set** discourse entity in terms of the same factors as for an independent existential.

Recall now that a sentence such as 56 (repeated below)

56. Wendy gave each girl Bruce knows a crayon.

can also be viewed from a prototype perspective. (e.g. "**She** used it to draw a Christmas card for her mother". cf. Section 2.5.) From this perspective, the ID-rule will identify e_3 as "the prototype girl Bruce knows" and e_4 as "the crayon mentioned in sentence 56 which Wendy gave to e_3". e_3's **ID** can be written as

[56-iv] x:G

(That is, I will use a notation in which the semantics assigned to restricted free variables is "prototype".) e_4's ID can be written as

[56-v] iy: C y & Gave e_2,e_3,y & **evoke** S_{56},y

Again, one term comes from the quantifier class restriction, one term comes from from the main predication and one term links discourse entity and sentence. Notice that this is the same **ID** as would be formed if sentence 56 was actually phrased in terms of the definite noun phrase - "Wendy gave a crayon to **the** prototypical girl Bruce knows".

Finally notice the similarity of the **IDs** formed in the set and prototype cases.

e_3 x:G
   ix:**maxset**(G)x

e_4 iy: Cy & Gave e_2,e_3,y & **evoke** S_{56},y
   iw:**maxset**$(\lambda(y)[Cy$ & $(Ex\epsilon e_3)$. Gave e_2,x,y & **evoke** $S_{56},y])w$

This implies that a system could assign a discourse entity a vague, temporary ID from which either of these IDs could be derived if and when the speaker's perspective were determined. <*33>

4.2 Independent Quantifiers and Definite Descriptions <*34>

This section presents a case by case summary (with brief examples) of the ID-rule, as it applies to independent quantifiers and definite descriptions. For each case, its structural description (SD) is given, followed by the **ID** of the discourse entity so evoked. F_x represents an arbitrary open sentence in which the variable x is free; C represents an arbitrary predicate on individuals and **K**, an arbitrary predicate on sets. ! marks the left end of a clause, and S_j is the label of clause j. Optional terms in the structural description are indicated in angle brackets. (Recall that after the ID-rule has applied to the leftmost term, a new interpretation will be formed in terms of the new discourse entity and the ID-rule re-applied.)

<*33>. One possibility for such a temporary ID would be the right-hand side of the prototype ID - i.e.,

G --> PROTOTYPE - x:G
      SET - ix:**maxset**(G)x

Cy & Gave e_2,e_3,y & **evoke** S_{56},y -->
   PROTOTYPE iy: Cy & Gave e_2,e_3,y & **evoke** S_{56},y
   SET - iw: **maxset**(λ(y)[Cy & (Ex e_3) . Gave e_2,x,y & **evoke** S_{56},y])w
<*34>. A reader who just wants to catch the gist of this chapter might go on to Section 5, thereby avoiding the technical details in Sections 4.2-4.4.

Case 1: Independent Existentials

SD: a. !(Ex:C) . F_x
      b. !(Ex:K) . F_x <& $|x|$=n>

entity: e_1

ID: a. ix: Cx & F_x & **evoke** S,x
      b. ix: Kx & F_x <& $|x|$=n> & **evoke** S,x

examples:

57. I saw a cat.
    (Ex:Cat) . Saw I,x

    e_1 ix: Cat x & Saw I,x & **evoke** S_{57},x
        "the just-mentioned cat I saw"

58. Three cats ate the pizza.
    (Ex:**set**(Cat)) . Ate x,iy:Pizza y & $|x|$=3

    e_1 ix: **set**(Cat)x & Ate x,iy:Pizza y & $|x|$=3 & **evoke** S_{58},x
    "the just-mentioned set of 3 cats who together ate the pizza"

comment:

   Recall that F_x is an open sentence. In the plural case, it may be
   of the form ($\forall$w $\in$ x) . F_w. That is, it is to be taken
   distributively. For example,

59. Three boys each caught an armadillo.
    (Ex:**set**(Boy))($\forall$w$\in$x)(Ey:A) . Caught w,y & $|x|$=3

    e_1 ix: **set**(Boy)x & ($\forall$w$\in$x)(Ey:A) . Caught w,y & $|x|$=3
        & **evoke** S_{59},x
        "the just-mentioned set of 3 boys, each of whom caught
        an armadillo"

Case 2: Definite Descriptions

SD: a. ix: Cx
      b. ix: Kx

entity: e_2

ID: a. ix: Cx
      b. ix: Kx

example:

60. I saw the cat which dislikes Sam.
    Saw I, ix:λ(u:Cat)[Dislike u, Sam]x

    e_2 ix:λ(u:Cat)[Dislike u, Sam]x
          "the cat which dislikes Sam"

example:

61. I saw the cats which dislike Sam.
    Saw I, ix: **maxset**(λ(u:Cat)[Dislike u, Sam])x

    e_2 ix: **maxset**(λ(u:Cat)[Dislike u, Sam])x
          "the cats which dislike Sam"

Case 3: Distributives

SD: a. !(∀x:C) . F$_x$
     b. !(∀x∈iw:Kw)^x. F$_x$

entity: e$_3$

ID:

  prototype
    a. x:C
    b. x∈iw:Kw

  set
    a. ix:**maxset(C)**x
    b. iw:**Kw**

example:

  62. Each cat that Wendy owns dislikes Sam.
     (∀x:λ(u:Cat)[Own Wendy,u]) . Dislike x,Sam

    e$_3$ x:λ(u:Cat)[Own Wendy,u]
        "the prototypical cat that Wendy owns"

        ix: **maxset**(λ(u:Cat)[Own Wendy,u])x
        "the set of cats that Wendy owns"

example:

  63. The three cats each scratched Sam.
     (∀w∈ix:**maxset**(Cat)x & |x|=3) . Scratched w, Sam

    e$_3$ w∈ix: **maxset**(Cat)x & |x|=3
        "the prototypical member of that set of three cats"

        ix: **maxset**(Cat)x & |x|=3
        "the three cats"

4.3 Dependent Quantifiers and Definite Descriptions

In any formula, dependencies between quantifiers alter in some way the **IDs** of their associated discourse entities. This was illustrated in Section 4.1, example 56, where a singular existential within the scope of a universal evoked a set-type discourse entity: alone it would have evoked an individual. There are three types of dependencies among quantifiers and definite descriptions that this ID-rule is sensitive to: (1) "for each...there exists" dependencies; (2) dependencies due to the class restriction of one quantifier referencing the variable bound by another; and (3) dependencies due to one quantifier occurring within another's class restriction. I shall take up each case in turn, showing how the rule operates to produce appropriate discourse entity **IDs**.

4.3.1 For each...there exists

Whenever an existential (either singular or plural) occurs within the scope of one or more distributive quantifiers, the **ID** of its associated discourse entity will depend on whether the distributives are viewed as prototypes or sets. Recall that when viewed prototypically, distributives behave like definite terms (i.e., "the prototypical x"). Since definite terms do not scope, the existential is essentially independent and Case 1 given above will apply. However when the distributives are viewed as evoking sets, both singular and plural existentials within their scope will evoke discourse entities describable as sets, each of whose members corresponds to one or more possible combinations of variable bindings over the distributives (cf. example 54 above). Likewise, when a distributive is viewed as evoking a set discourse entity, e_j, the interpretation it occurs in will be re-written in terms of e_j as $...(\forall x_j \in e_j)...$ and the term to its right processed next. <*35>

On the next pages Q_j stands for $(\forall x_j \in e_j)$ where e_j is the label of an earlier evoked set discourse entity, and F_y stands for an open sentence in which y and perhaps other variables are free.

<*35>. I shall not speculate on a mixed set/prototype perspective because it does not seem to be a real possibility.

Case 4: Distributively Quantified Existentials

SD: a. $!Q_1...Q_n$ (Ey:C) . F_y
b. $!Q_1...Q_n$ (Ey:K) . F_y^y <& $|y|=m$>

ID: a. iy:**maxset**$(\lambda(u:C)[(Ex_1 \epsilon e_1)...(Ex_n \epsilon e_n)$. F_u & **evoke** S,u])y
b. iy:**maxset**$(\lambda(u:K)[(Ex_1 \epsilon e_1)...(Ex_n \epsilon e_n)$. F_u <& $|u|=m$>
& **evoke** S,u])y

examples:

64. Each boy gave each girl a peach.
   $(\forall x:B)(\forall y:G)(Ez:P)$. Gave x,y,z

   e_1 ix: **maxset**(**B**)x
   e_2 iy: **maxset**(**G**)y
   e_3 iz: **maxset**$(\lambda(u:P)[(Ex \epsilon e_1)(Ey \epsilon e_2)$. Gave x,y,u
            & **evoke** S_{64},u])z
   "the set of peaches, each of which is linked to S_{64} by virtue
   of some member of e_1 giving it to some member of e_2"

65. Each boy gave each girl three peaches.
   $(\forall x:B)(Ey:G)(Ez:set(P))$. Gave x,y,z

   e_1 ix:**maxset**(**B**)x
   e_2 iy:**maxset**(**G**)y
   e_3 iz:**maxset**$(\lambda(u:set(P))[(Ex \epsilon e_1)(Ey \epsilon e_2)$. Gave x,y,u & $|u|=3$
            & **evoke** S_{65},u])z
   "the set of peach triplets, each of which is linked to S_{65} by
   virtue of some member of e_1 giving it to some member of e_2"

comments:

1. As I mentioned earlier, the discourse entity evoked by a plural
   existential can also be described as a set of individuals, cf.

   iz:**maxset**$(\lambda(w)[(Ex \epsilon e_1)(Ey \epsilon e_2)(Eu:set(P))$. wϵu
            & Gave x,y,u & **evoke** S,u])z

   This description can be derived simply from the one given above,
   and may be a more appropriate way of viewing the entity for
   resolving a subsequent definite anaphor, e.g. "Every one of **them**
   was rotten." Cardinality is optional here since there is no need
   for the set u to be either unique or maximal.

2. F_y will be of the form $(\forall w \epsilon y)$. F_w, if the plural existential is
   to be taken distributively. For example,

   66. Each boy paid for each of three peaches.
      $(\forall x:B)(Ey:\textbf{set}(P))(\forall w \epsilon y)$. Paid-for x,w & $|y|=3$

      e_1 ix:**maxset**(**B**)x
      e_2 iz:**maxset**$(\lambda(u:\textbf{set}(P))[(Ex \epsilon e_1)(\forall w \epsilon u)$. Paid-for x,w & $|u|=3$
               & **evoke** S_{66},u])z
      "the just-mentioned set of peach triplets, each of which is
      linked to S_{66} by some boy paying for each of its members"

4.3.2 Class Restriction Dependencies

The fact that English has relative clauses and possessive determiners means that another type of dependency between terms is possible. In a Level-2 representation, this dependency is visible as a variable in a term's class restriction, where the variable is bound either **directly** by a distributive or **indirectly** by a quantifier whose class restriction depends on a distributive.   Since unlike a "for each...there exists" dependency, this dependency is not restricted to existentials, it is possible for the **ID** of a discourse entity evoked by a universal or a definite description to be affected by context as well. Before presenting the relevant cases of the ID-rule, I shall illustrate class restriction dependencies with two examples.

Consider the following sentence
67. Every boy gave a girl he knew the peach she wanted.
One possibility is that "he" stands for the variable bound by the quantifier associated with "every boy" and "she", for the one associated with "a girl he knew". This possibility translates into the following Level-2 representation.

[67-i] $(\forall x:B)(Ey:\lambda(u:G)[\mathbf{K}\ x,u])$. Gave $x,y,iz:\lambda(v:P)[\mathbf{W}\ y,v]z$
(where **B** stands for "boy", **G**, for "girl", **K**, for "knew", **P**, for "peach", and **W** for "wanted"). <*36>

Applying the ID-rule to [67-i], the first discourse entity evoked, say e_1, would be identified as "the set of boys". Re-writing [67-i] in terms of e_1 - i.e.,

[67-ii] $(\forall x \in e_1)(Ey:\lambda(u:G)[\mathbf{K}\ x,u])$. Gave $x,y,iz:\lambda(v:P)[\mathbf{W}\ y,v]z$
and re-applying the ID-rule identifies the second discourse entity, say e_2, as

iy:**maxset**$(\lambda(u:Girl)[(Ex \in e_1)$. $\mathbf{K}\ x,u$
& Gave $x,u,iz:\lambda(v:P)[\mathbf{W}\ u,v]z$ & **evoke** $S_{67},u])y$
"the set of girls, each of whom some member of e_1 who knew her
gave the peach she wanted"

<*36>. If the pronouns were resolved against discourse entities, the **ID** of the existentially evoked entity would follow from Case 4 above (if set perspective) or Case 1 (if prototype). The **ID** of the discourse entity evoked by the definite description would follow from Case 2.

and the third discourse entity, e_3 as
        iz:**maxset**$(\lambda(u)[(Ey\epsilon e_2) \ . \ u=\hat{\imath}w:\lambda(v:P)[W \ y,v]w])z$
        "the set of peaches, each of which was the peach that some
        member of e_2 wanted"

Notice that binding an existential **explicitly** within the scope of a
distributive through its class restriction does not affect the **ID** of the
existentially evoked entity any more than just being within the scope of
the universal. However, binding a definite description in this way
does. The entity evoked by a singular definite description, as in the
example above, is describable as a set rather than as an individual.
<*37>

This behavior only arises through class restriction dependencies on
a distributive viewed as a set. Binding a term explicitly within the
scope of an independent existential or a distributive viewed
prototypically (i.e., similar to a definite description) does not affect
the **ID** of the discourse entity the term evokes. For example,

  68. Bruce gave a girl he knew the peach she wanted.
Assuming "he" refers to the same discourse entity, say e_1, that "Bruce"
does and "she" stands for the variable bound by $(Ey:...)$, the Level-2
representation of sentence 68 is

  [68-i] $(Ey:\lambda(u:G)[K \ PRO=e_1,u]) \ . \ Gave \ e_1,y,iz:\lambda(v:P)[W \ y,v]z$
Intuitively, the other two discourse entities evoked by this sentence
can be described as "the just-mentioned girl whom e_1 knew to whom he
gave the peach she wanted" and "the peach that girl wanted". (Call
these e_2 and e_3, respectively.) From [68-i], e_2 would be identified as
  e_2 iy:$\lambda(u:G)[K \ e_1,u]y \ \& \ Gave \ e_1,y,iz:\lambda(v:P)[W \ y,v]z$
        & **evoke** S_{68},y
        "the just-mentioned girl whom e_1 knew to whom he gave the peach
        she wanted"

<*37>. There is another way of describing e_3 uniquely - i.e.,

        iz:**maxset**$(\lambda(u)[(Ey\epsilon e_2) \ . \ \lambda(v:P)[W \ y,v]u])z$
"the set of peaches such that some member of e_2 wanted that peach."
That is, it is not necessary to assert the uniqueness of each peach in
the description since it is guaranteed by sentence 67 being true.
However, this redundancy may make for greater efficiency and I would
suggest keeping it.

Re-writing [68-i] in terms of e_2 yields

   [68-ii] Gave $e_1,e_2,iz:\lambda(v:P)[\textbf{W} \ y,e_2]z$

Since the definite term is now not scoped by any quantifiers, Case 2 above applies to produce the following ID for e_3

   $e_3 \quad iz:\lambda(v:P)[\textbf{W} \ e_2,v]z$

    I shall now present those cases of the ID-rule which apply to terms whose class restrictions depend either directly or indirectly on a distributive. (Since existentials are covered by earlier cases, this will be limited to distributives and definite terms.) As for notation, Q_j will stand for the jth quantifier of an expression, and x_j is the variable it binds. <*38> C represents a class restriction on individuals and K, a class restriction on sets. Class restriction dependencies on variables $x_{j1}...x_{jk}$ (where for all i, $1 \leqslant j_i \leqslant n$, $j_i < j_{i+1}$) will be indicated as $C(x_{j1}...x_{jk})$ or $K(x_{j1}...x_{jk})$, as appropriate. This should be taken to mean that the class restriction is either directly or indirectly dependent on these k variables. F_y represents an open sentence in which y and perhaps other variables are free. P represents an arbitrary predicate.

<*38>. Q_1 will be a distributive, since each of the independent existentials originally to its left in the Level-2 representation will have been replaced with a pointer to its corresponding discourse entity.

Case 5: Class Dependent Definite Descriptions

SD: a. $!Q_1...Q_n$. P iy:$C(x_{j1}...x_{jk})y$
      b. $!Q_1...Q_n$. P iy:$K(x_{j1}...x_{jk})y$ <& $|y|$=n>

entity: e_y

ID: a. iy:**maxset**$(\lambda(u)[(Ex_{j1}\in e_{j1})...(Ex_{jk}\in e_{jk})$
         . $u=iw:C(x_{j1}...x_{jk})w])\overline{y}$
      b. iy:**maxset**$(\lambda(u)[(Ex_{j1}\in e_{j1})...(Ex_{jk}\in e_{jk})$
         . $u=iw:K(x_{j1}...x_{jk})w$ <& $|w|$=n>])y

example: <*39>

69. Each boy gave a woman he knew the two peaches she desired.

    ** assuming the pronouns stand for bound variables **

    $(\forall x:B)(Ey:\lambda(u:W)[K\ x,u])$. G x,y,iz:set(P)z & D y,z
    & $|z|$=2

  e_1 ix:**maxset**(B)x
          "the set of boys"

  e_2 iy:**maxset**$(\lambda(u)[(Ex\in e_1)$.$\lambda(v:W)[K\ x,v]u$
          & G x,u,iz:**set**(P)z & D u,z & $|z|$=2 & **evoke** S_{69},u])y
          "the set of women, each of whom is associated with S_{69} by
          virtue of some member of e_1 who knew her having given her the
          two peaches she desired"

  e_3 iz:**maxset**$(\lambda(u)[(Ey\in e_2)$. u=iw:set(P)w & D y,w & $|w|$=2])z
          "the set of pairs of peaches, each of which was the pair that
          some member of e_2 desired"

- -

Case 6: Class Dependent Distributives

SD: a. $!Q_1...Q_n(\forall y:C(x_{j1}...x_{jk}))$. F_y
      b. $!Q_1...Q_n(\forall y\in iw:K(x_{j1}...x_{kj}))$. F_y

entity: e_y

ID: a. iy:**maxset**$(\lambda(u)[(Ex_{j1}\in e_{j1})...(Ex_{jk}\in e_{jk})$. $C(x_{j1}...x_{jk})u])y$
      b. iy:**maxset**$(\lambda(u)[(Ex_{j1}\in e_{j1})...(Ex_{jk}\in e_{jk})$
         . $u\in iw:K(x_{j1}...x_{jk})w])y$

example:

70. Every boy I know loves every woman he meets.

    ** assuming the pronoun stands for a bound variable **

    $(\forall x:B)(\forall y:\lambda(u:W)[Meet\ x,u])$. L x,y

      e_1 ix:**maxset**(B)x
      e_2 iy:**maxset**$(\lambda(u)[(Ex\in e_1)$. $\lambda(v:W)[Meet\ x,v]u])y$
              "the set of women, each of whom some member of e_1 has met"

<*39>. For a singular definite description, see Example 67 earlier.

4.3.3 Quantifiers in Class Restrictions

As I discussed in Section 2.6, a special case of the ID-rule is needed to accommodate parameterized individuals: while they are not "real" entities which can be referred to later in the discourse, they can be referred to intra-sententially. First note that a parameterized individual will be evoked whenever a noun phrase embedded in a relative clause interprets into an existential quantifier or a term whose class restriction depends on the variable bound by the relative clause (cf. Section 3.1). Other noun phrases, even in a relative clause, will evoke or refer to "real" discourse entities. For example, compare the following sentence pairs.

71. Everyone who fed **the cat** gave it too much. It has gotten very fat.
72. Everyone who fed **a cat** gave it too much. They have gotten very fat.

In the first pair, both "it"'s refer to the same discourse entity as "the cat". In the second pair, "it" refers to an entity describable as "the cat s/he fed" where "s/he" stands for the variable bound by "everyone" ($\forall$). As such, it cannot be referenced outside the scope of "everyone". <*40>

Recall from Section 3 that I am assuming that the process of converting from a Level-1 into a Level-2 interpretation starts from the leftmost, most embedded clause. Given the way an **ID** is formed for an existentially-evoked entity (Case 1) or one evoked by a class dependent definite (Case 5) or distributive (Case 6), if the ID-rule were applied to a relative clause containing such a term, the **ID** of the entity it evoked would contain the variable bound by the relative clause. For example, consider applying Case 1 of the ID-rule to the embedded clause in

---

<*40>. In a situation like
    Everyone who fed a cat gave it too much.
    It has gotten very fat.
one has to make the additional assumption that the speaker believes that everyone fed the same cat ("it"), although the presense of several cats makes it impossible to use "the cat" in the first sentence.

73. Every man who owns a donkey beats it.

$(\forall x:\lambda(u:M)[(Ey:D)$. Own u,y]) . Beat x,IT

The entity associated with the existential term would be identified as

iy: Dy & Own u,y & **evoke** $S_{73.1}$,u
"the just-mentioned donkey that u owns"

Recall from Section 3.1 that the semantics of restricted quantification is such that the variable of quantification, here x, satisfies the predicate in the Q-restriction. Thus if x satisfies $\lambda(u:M)[(Ey:D)$. Own u,y], it follows that there is an entity identifiable as

iy: Dy & Own x,y & **evoke** $S_{73.1}$,y
"the donkey x owns"

This is a valid **ID** for a parameterized individual within the scope of $(\forall x:...)$, and thus a possible referent for "it", i.e.

$(\forall x:\lambda(u:M)[(Ey:D)$. Own u,y]) . Beat x, iy: Dy & Own x,y
& **evoke** $S_{73.1}$,y
"Every man who owns a donkey beats the donkey he owns"

As a second example, consider

74. No woman who loves the cat she owns beats it.

Assuming that "she" stands for the variable bound by the relative clause predicate, the Level-2 representation of the sentence is

$\sim(Ex:\lambda(u:W)[Love u,iy:\lambda(v:C)[Own u,v]y])$. Beat x,IT

If Case 5 of the ID-rule were applied to its embedded clause, the entity associated with the definite term would be identified as

iy:$\lambda(v:C)[Own u,v]y$
"the cat u owns"

Again, if x satisfies the predicate $\lambda(u:W)[Love u,...]$, it follows that there is an entity describable as

iy:$\lambda(v:C)[Own x,v]y$
"the cat x owns"

This is a valid **ID** for a parameterized individual within the scope of $(Ex:...)$ and thus a possible referent for "it", cf.

$\sim(Ex:\lambda(u:W)[Love u,iy:\lambda(v:C)[Own u,v]y])$
. Beat x,iy:$\lambda(v:C)[Own x,v]y$
"No woman who loves the cat she owns beats the cat she owns"

As far as the actual discourse entities evoked by these embedded noun phrases, their **IDs** follow directly from Case 5 (i.e., Class

Dependent Definites). To see this, notice that the **ID** of a parameterized individual, like all **ID**s, is definite and is always within the scope of, and thus dependent on, the matrix quantifier. If one acts as if this dependent definite is explicitly in the matrix, then by applying Case 5 to it, an appropriate discourse entity and its **ID** fall right out.

Notice that I am advocating forming an **ID** for a parameterized individual independent of whether or not it is referenced intra-sententially: the "real" discourse entity may still be referenced later on. For example,

75a. Every man in Boston who owns a donkey is a capitalist.
$(\forall x:\lambda(u:M)[(Ey:D) . Own\ u,y]) . C\ x$
   b. **The donkeys** however are Marxists and are planning to revolt.

(**M** stands for "man in Boston", **D**, for "donkey" and **C**, for "capitalist"). The existential in the embedded clause (labelled $S_{75a.1}$) evokes a parameterized individual which can be described as "the just-mentioned donkey he owns".

iy: D y & Own x,y & evoke $S_{75a.1}$,y

If the universally quantified noun phrase is viewed as a set,

e_1 ix:**maxset**(**M**)x

i.e., "the set of men in Boston", Case 5 of the ID-rule will apply to identify the actual discourse entity as

iz:**maxset**$(\lambda(u)[(Ex\in e_1) . u = iy: Dy\ \&\ Own\ x,y]\ \&\ evoke\ S_{75a.1},y])z$

i.e., "the set of donkeys, each of which is the just-mentioned donkey which some member of e_1 owns". This is the referent of "the donkeys" in sentence 75b.

5. Other Factors in Deriving Descriptions

I am aware of having omitted several factors to which a truly adequate ID-rule must be sensitive. These are discussed here briefly.

5.1 Tense

Tense is an important component of the IDs of discourse entities,
be they individuals, sets or quantities of stuff. The reason why can be
seen by comparing such examples as

76a. Bruce built a throne to replace his old one.
  b. He will use it when he is crowned emperor (but then he won't use
     it again).
77a. Bruce will build a throne to replace his old one.
  b. He used it when he was crowned emperor (and doesn't want to use
     it again).

In example 76, there are two possible referents for "it": the discourse
entity describable as "the throne Bruce built to replace his old one
mentioned in sentence 76b" - and that describable as "Bruce's old
throne". (The former seems more plausible, but whether that is
attributable to the semantics of "replace" or to a syntactic focus
effect - a discourse entity evoked by a main clause noun phrase is more
salient than one evoked by an embedded noun phrase - is not clear.)
Similarly in example 77, there are two possible referents for "it", but
only one is plausible - that describable as "Bruce's old throne".   The
other possible referent - that describable as "the throne Bruce will
build to replace his old one, mentioned in sentence 77b." - can be
rejected on the grounds that one can't have already used an entity that
is yet to be built. On the other hand, one can use in the future an
entity that was built in the past. The only conclusion is that to apply
such real world knowledge as this in resolving anaphora requires an
adequate indication of tense in discourse entity IDs.

Another kind of example which makes a somewhat different demand on
an adequate indication of tense involves contemporaneous states and/or
events, e.g.

78. Bill will marry a woman who loves Bruce.

The problem is whether the existentially evoked entity should be
described as "the woman whom Bill will marry, who loves Bruce now, who
was mentioned in sentence 78" or as "the woman whom Bill will marry, who
will love Bruce when Bill marries her, who was mentioned in sentence
78". However even if the the listener cannot decide between them

immediately, it may be that it is only possible to resolve a subsequent
definite anaphor against this discourse entity if one or the other **ID** is
correct.   Thus the derivation of appropriate discourse entity **ID**s must
be sensitive to indications of contemporaneity, as well as temporal
order.

5.2 Conditionals

Another factor which affects what **ID** is appropriate for the
discourse entity evoked by an indefinite noun phrase is whether it
occurs in a conditional context. For example,

79. **If** Wendy has **a cat**, it is a Burmese.

80. **If** I buy **some cats**, I shall bring them home.

Now intuitively, the "it" in sentence 79 refers to the discourse
entity describable as "the just-mentioned cat that Wendy has if Wendy
has a cat".   In sentence 80, "them" refers to the discourse entity
describable as "the just-mentioned set of cats that I will buy (or will
have bought) if I buy some cats". The important point is that these
discourse entities must not be treated as "existing" in the same sense
as ones evoked in non-conditional contexts, e.g.

81. Wendy has a cat.

The cat mentioned in sentence 81 - "the just-mentioned cat that Wendy
has" - can be the referent of "it" in a subsequent sentence like

Yesterday it ate a hole in my sweater.

However, the cat mentioned in sentence 79 - "the just-mentioned cat that
Wendy has if Wendy has a cat" - can not. Thus for a discourse entity ID
to be appropriate, it must be able to reflect conditional contexts.
<*41>

<*41>. Notice that the definite pronouns in examples 79 and 80 can not
be treated as bound variables (cf. Chapter 1, Section 5). That is,
sentence 79 can not be interpreted as

$\quad$ (∀x:Cat) . Have Wendy x, ==> Burmese x

i.e., "for any cat, if Wendy has it, it is a Burmese". Doing so leads
to the following problem.   By the ID-rule, any sentence containing a
wide scope universal is associated with a set discourse entity which can
be referenced subsequently with a definite anaphor. For example,

82a. Every cat at BBN loves asparagus.

$\quad$ (∀x:λ(u:Cat)[At u,BBN]) . Love x, Asparagus

5.3 Disjunction

Disjunction, either clausal or phrasal, explicit or implicit, can
affect what **ID** is appropriate for a discourse entity in a way that
conjunction cannot. Consider the following sentences, the first two of
which come from [Karttunen, 1977].

83. If Wendy has a car or Bruce has a bike, **it** will be in the
    garage.

84. Bruce can choose between a bike and a car, but he must keep **it**
    in the garage.

85. Either Bruce has a new car or he has borrowed his brother's. In
    any case, **it** is blocking my driveway.

86. Whether Bruce buys a car or his brother buys a bike, he will
    have to keep **it** in the garage.

One way of looking at these sentences is that each term of the
disjunction evokes a different discourse entity into   the   listener's
model, each with a different ID:

(83) "the car that Wendy has (if she has a car)"
     "the bike that Bruce has (if he has a bike)"

(84) "the bike that Bruce will have (if he chooses a bike)"
     "the car that Bruce will have (if he chooses a car)"

(85) "the new car that Bruce has (if Bruce has a new car)"
     "Bruce's brother's car"

(86) "the car Bruce will have bought (if he buys a car)"
     "the bike Bruce's brother will have bought (if Bruce's brother
     buys a bike)"

The truth of the disjunction (which seems in each case to be interpreted
as exclusive "or") then guarantees there being one and only one entity
in the model to which "it" refers.   Notice that if the terms were

---

b. **They** also love cheese.
   they = the set of cats at BBN
If a conditional sentence like 79 is interpreted as having a wide scope
universal, a set discourse entity will be evoked. But that is not
correct. For example,

79. If Wendy has a cat, it is a Burmese. *She probably got **them** from
    Bill.
    them = ??

I propose the following simple Level-1 representation for conditional
sentences like 79 and 80.

    if (Ex:Cat) . Have Wendy,x **then** Burmese IT
    if (Ex:**set**(Cat)) . Buy I,x **then** Bring I, THEY, "home"

conjoined rather than disjoined, the truth of the conjunction would imply the simultaneous existence of two entities within the model. In that case, either the referent of "it" would be ambiguous or the sentence would just be bizarre.

I see another approach to these sentences, which is unique to disjunction. This holds that a **single** entity is evoked into the model, with the indecision (i.e., the disjunction) embodied in its **ID**. That **ID** is of the form "A if P, otherwise B". For example, the entity evoked by sentence 83 is describable as "the car that Wendy has (if she has a car) or the bike that Bruce has otherwise"; that evoked by sentence 84 is describable as "the bike that Bruce will have (if he chooses a bike) or the car that Bruce will have otherwise"; that evoked by sentence 85, as "the new car that Bruce has (if he has a new car) or Bruce's brother's car otherwise"; and that evoked by sentence 86, as "the car Bruce will have bought (if he buys a car) or the bike Bruce's brother will have bought otherwise".

One advantage to this approach is that additional properties which truthfully follow from either **ID** can be ascribed to the entity without committing oneself either way. This can be useful in anaphor resolution. For example, in sentence 85, the subject of "block my driveway" must be a physical object, preferably large and somewhat mobile. This condition is satisfied by the discourse entity evoked by sentence 85, independent of which **ID** is appropriate. Taking this approach means that for discourse entity **IDs** to be appropriate, they must be sensitive to disjunctive contexts.

5.4 Negation

As might be expected, general propositional negation creates a problem for the derivation of discourse entities, in that the ID-rule given in Section 4 does not hold in any simple way. For example, consider the sentence

87. Bruce didn't marry a Swedish girl.
    $\sim(Ex:\lambda(u:Girl)[Swedish\ u])$. Marry Bruce, x

which in its neutral sense holds that "it is not true that Bruce married a Swedish girl". There are several more specific ways of understanding sentence 87, each of which will evoke an individual discourse entity with a somewhat different **ID** (or else no individual discourse entity at all). Consider the following continuations of sentence 87.

88a. He is just living with **her**.
   b. **She** is from Denmark.
   c. **She** is at least 15 years his senior.
   d. **The bride** was, rather, a very attractive boy.
   e. As far as I know, he's still single.

On the one hand, sentence 88e. shows that no discourse entity should be created in response to sentence 87. On the other hand, for sentences 88a-d an appropriate **ID** can be formed by postulating a narrower scope for negation than the whole clause. <*42> For example, sentence 88a. assumes that NEG ($\tilde{\ }$) just scopes the predicate symbol in 87. This might be represented explicitly in a second-order predicate calculus as

$$(E\mathcal{G})(Ex:\lambda(u:Girl)[Swedish\ u])\ .\ \mathcal{G}\ Bruce,x\ \&\ \mathcal{G} \neq Marry$$

<*43> As such, sentence 87 evokes an entity describable as "the just-mentioned Swedish girl whom Bruce participates in some other relation with than 'marry'". Sentence 88a. says that relation is "living with".

Example 88b. follows from interpreting sentence 87 as saying that Bruce married a girl and that the just-mentioned girl that Bruce married is not Swedish. That is, the first assertion

$$(Ex:Girl)\ .\ Married\ Bruce,x$$

evokes a discourse entity (say e_1) which can be described as "the just-mentioned girl whom Bruce married". The second assertion, with NEG scoping "Swedish",

$$\tilde{\ }Swedish\ e_1$$

<*42>. In oral discourse, stress can be used to indicate such a narrow scope, thereby eliminating the current problem. However, my concern is with written discourse, in which sentences like 87 are truly ambiguous.
<*43>. There is also an invited inference that $\mathcal{G}$ is similar, but not equivalent to Marry.

denies that she is Swedish. (Sentence 88b. goes on to inform the listener that she is from Denmark.) Again the point is that a discourse entity **is** evoked, but its **ID** is not the same as would come from a positive context.

Sentences 88c&d can be analyzed in a way similar to sentence 88b. Sentence 88c. follows from interpreting sentence 87 as saying that (1) Bruce married a Swedish female and (2) the just-mentioned Swedish female that Bruce married is not a girl. (That is, NEG scopes that component of "girl" relating to youth.) Sentence 88c. then asserts that she is at least 15 years older than he. Finally sentence 88d. assumes that sentence 87 is saying that (1) Bruce married a Swedish person and (2) the just-mentioned Swedish person that Bruce married is not a female. (That is, NEG just scopes the female component of "girl".) Sentence 88d. then asserts this latter claim explicitly.

An adequate treatment of this problem of incrementing a discourse model appropriately in response to explicit (but ambiguous) negation should take into account at least the following observations. First, no matter what scope NEG may later be assumed to have, the description "Swedish girl" must still be available as an antecedent for "one"-anaphora (cf. Chapter 3, Section 6). For example,

89a. Bruce didn't marry a Swedish girl.
  b. She was from Denmark.
  c. However, Fred married **one** and is very happy he did.
     one = Swedish girl

The second observation is that a cooperative speaker tends to clarify immediately an utterance s/he knows to be ambiguous. (This is captured as one of Grices's "Maxims of Manner" [Grice, 1975].) A sentence such as 87. will generally be followed by a sentence like 88a-e, to make clear what was meant. <*44>

Thus a system could adopt the strategy of assigning an explicitly negative sentence a Level-1 representation in terms of full propositional negation and then not processing it for discourse entities

---

<*44>. The intentional use of two sentences in this way, rather than a single unambiguous sentence, serves a variety of rhetorical purposes, including suspense, contrast, etc.

immediately. If soon after that, the need arose to resolve a definite anaphor, the ID-rule could be applied to the proposition inside the scope of ~, with the knowledge that at least one piece of the **ID** so produced would be wrong. Which piece that was would have to be determined with respect to the sentence containing the anaphor. For example, consider sentence 88b. again - "She was from Denmark". Resolving "she" against the discourse entity tentatively describable as "the just-mentioned Swedish girl that Bruce married" and knowing that part of that **ID** was wrong, would allow one (given the appropriate assumptions) to eliminate "Swedish". <*45>

The point of this is that negation affects discourse model synthesis in subtle ways. While full propositional negation is truth-functionally correct, it is too vague to be of use in identifying the speaker-intended discourse entities. However since it may be impossible for the listener to determine the intended scope of negation immediately, this is another case where the act of resolving a subsequent anaphoric expression may contribute to resolving a standing ambiguity.

(Notice that a belief context poses much the same problem as negation - that of determining its scope. For example, in
> 91. Bruce thought he married a Swedish girl, but **she** was really from Denmark.

"she" refers to the just-mentioned girl that Bruce married. It is only the modifier "Swedish" that is in the scope of belief.)

6. Discourse Models and Anaphor Resolution

To close this chapter on definite pronoun anaphora, I shall give two examples which illustrate the process of synthesizing a discourse model from a text and which show how it complements the process of resolving definite anaphora. I shall begin with the simple case of an

---

<*45>. Such assumptions may require not only semantic and factual knowledge, but knowledge of the speaker's beliefs as well, e.g.
> 90. Bruce didn't marry a Swedish girl. **She** was a brunette.

Here the speaker may intend "she" to refer to the just-mentioned girl that Bruce married, believing all Swedes to be blondes.

unambiguous sentence and then note how this is complicated by definite anaphora which must themselves be resolved.

First, a brief outline (illustrated schematically in Figure 1). As each sentence of a discourse comes into the system, it is labelled according to its sequential place in the discourse (e.g. S_{10}) and parsed following some simple conventions of $\overline{X}$ syntax [Jackendoff, 1977]. <*46> (If the sentence contains any embedded clauses, those clauses will be assigned labels reflecting their sequence in the sentence as well - e.g. $S_{10.1}$, $S_{10.2.1}$, etc.) Each distinct parse tree resulting from this step (given the fairly loose specifications noted in footnote 46) is passed to an interpreter to determine its Level-1 representation. <*47> If a

---

<*46>. I expect this parse tree to show the major syntactic constituents: noun phrase (NP), verb phrase (VP), embedded sentence (S), prepositional phrase (PP), nominal (NOM - i.e., the core of the noun phrase without its determiner) and auxiliary (AUX). Passives are not to be "undone", as it would complicate an adequate treatment of verb phrase ellipsis (cf. Chapter 4, Sections 2.1 & 2.3). Moreover, undoing passives may require extra-syntactic information to be done correctly. (Voice - active/passive - however must be noted as part of the auxiliary since verb phrase ellipsis is sensitive to voice.) I do not require that word senses be disambiguated except insofar as different word senses imply different syntactic structures. I do not require that pre-nominal modifiers (adjectives and nouns) be arranged in a structure which reflects their semantic roles. I do not require that prepositional phrases be hung off the "correct" node: a table of possibilities is sufficient (cf. the "well-formed substring table" used in LUNAR [Woods et al. 1972]). This means that a parser such as LUNAR's would be capable of producing the kind of parse tree I minimally expect. If a parser does have access to other knowledge in the form of a semantic or pragmatic grammar [Burton 1976; Woods et al. 1975] or in the form of hooks into the lexicon [Bates & Bobrow, 1978] and can therefore produce a representation in which word senses are disambiguated, etc., that simply means less work for the interpretation procedure, to be discussed next. (Since I haven't thought at all about conjunction vis a vis deriving discourse entities and their appropriate descriptions, I cannot say what I would expect of a parser in this regard.)

<*47>. Recall from Section 3 that a Level-1 representation reflects at least the following:
   a. the case structure of each verb (indicated here as a predicate and its arguments)
   b. the number and specificity of each noun phrase
   c. quantifier scope (wherever possible)

Anaphoric expressions are still around explicitly in a Level-1 representation (e.g. HE, IT, P? - for ellipsed verb phrases, cf.

parse tree cannot be so interpreted, it will be discarded as nonsensical.

Each distinct Level-1 representation of the original sentence is then passed to a second interpreter to determine its Level-2 representation. Starting from the leftmost, most deeply embedded clause, this conversion process involves finding antecedents for any ellipsed verb phrases; <*48> resolving any definite pronouns or at least identifying whether a bound variable or parameterized individual interpretation <*49> is possible; for each definite description, deciding whether it is anaphoric or not <*50> and if so, replacing it with the label of its discourse entity referent; resolving quantifier scope ambiguities; for relative clauses, forming IDs for any parameterized individuals so evoked (cf. Section 4.3.3), etc. It is possible for one Level-1 representation to be ambiguous vis a vis its Level-2 interpretation and for another one to have no Level-2 interpretations at all. If only a single Level-2 interpretation is possible, the ID-rule will be applied to it to identify the new discourse entities that have been evoked. If several Level-2 interpretations are possible, the application of the ID-rule can be delayed until the need arises to resolve a definite anaphor. <*51> The

Chapter 4). The production of such a representation is within the current capabilities of semantic interpretation programs such as those used in LUNAR [Woods et al., 1972] and PHLIQA [Medema et al., 1976].
<*48>. What is needed for resolving ellipsed verb phrases is laid out in Chapter 4.
<*49>. Insofar as resolving definite anaphora (both definite pronouns and definite descriptions) involves consistency checking, that part of the process can be carried out to the extent that an "inference engine" can be devised. Insofar as it involves constraining the number of alternative hypotheses that have to be checked and weighed against each other, that part of the process is currently being investigated by several people already mentioned, including Bullwinkle [1977], Grosz [1977] and Hobbs [1976a&b].
<*50>. It may be impossible at this point to determine whether a definite noun phrase is anaphoric or not. For example, it may contain as yet unresolvable definite pronouns whose referents would make a difference as to whether the definite noun phrase itself were anaphoric. The listener's failure to detect a noun phrase as being anaphoric means that s/he will have two distinct discourse entities, where the speaker has only one. This may lead to misunderstandings.
<*51>. At that point, one can probably use any known constraints on the

Figure 1

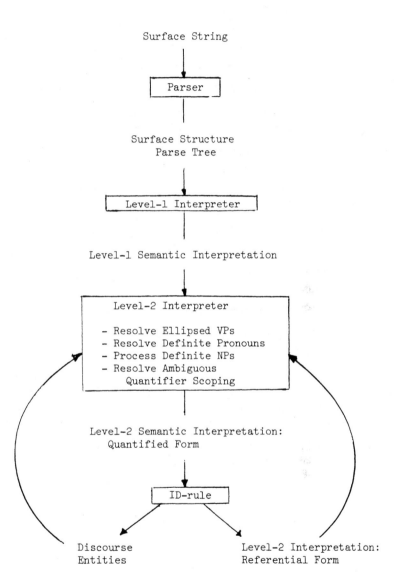

ID-rule will be applied to the leftmost quantifier or definite description, identifying and labelling the new discourse entity it evokes (e.g. e_{14}, e_{15}, etc.), forming a new referential form of the Level-2 representation in terms of that entity, and then repeating the procedure for the next term. The discourse entities so produced will then be available for anaphoric reference later in the discourse. <*52>

I said earlier that I have not concerned myself with how a discourse model should be organized in order to facilitate anaphor resolution. Some techniques that have been proposed were discussed in Chapter 1, Section 3.2. For now, I shall just assume some reasonable organization, even if it is only a simple history list (cf. Woods et al. [1972], Winograd [1972], Brown & Burton [1975]).

I shall now give a simple example which illustrates this discourse model synthesis. Suppose that the next sentence of an on-going discourse is

92. Bruce found a banana.

As it comes into the system, it will be labelled, say, S_{92}, and parsed into the surface structure tree

```
S NP NPR Bruce
  AUX TENSE past
      VOICE active
  VP V find
     NP DET ART a
        NOM N banana
        NU singular
```

This will be interpreted into a Level-1 representation reflecting, **inter alia,** the case structure of the verb, the number and specificity of each noun phrase, etc.

---

anaphor's possible referent to select which of the Level-2 interpretations to process for discourse entities and hence for candidate referents. However I think it will be clearer just what an efficient response to multiple interpretations will be, when the scheme presented here for discourse model synthesis and anaphor resolution is implemented.

<*52>. As I mentioned in Chapter 1, Section 5, other discourse entities evoked by the discourse participants' shared spatio-temporal context will be available as well. (See also Nash-Webber [1977].) My concern here is only with textually evoked discourse entities.

(i)   (Ex:Banana) . Found Bruce,x

(Recall that I am finessing the problem of representing temporal context, partially conveyed by tense). This Level-1 representation will then be converted into a Level-2 representation. In the current case, this will involve identifying whether or not the definite description "Bruce" refers to some earlier evoked discourse entity, say e_{43}. If it does, it will be replaced by the label of that discourse entity, producing the Level-2 representation

(ii)   (Ex:Banana) . Found e_{43},x

If the definite description "Bruce" is not anaphoric, the Level-2 representation will be equivalent to its Level-1 representation.

The ID-rule will then be applied to the Level-2 representation (either (i) or (ii)) to produce the following discourse entity (or entities).

$[e_{44}$
EGO   ix: Banana x & Found e_{43},x & **evoke** S_{92},x]

(and if (i) is the Level-2 representation,

$[e_{45}$
EGO   Bruce]   .)

Here the information about an entity is indicated on its property list, with its ID hanging off an "EGO link", cf. [Woods, 1975]. (Obviously more sophisticated, structured descriptions of these discourse entities (a la KRL [Bobrow & Winograd, 1977] or SI-Net1 [Brachman, 1978]) are also possible. I am only giving minimal requirements in order to focus more on the interaction of discourse model synthesis and anaphor resolution.) Finally sentence S_{92} will be tagged with both its Level-2 interpretation and the entities it is associated with.

$[S_{92}$
INTERP   (Ex:Banana) . Found Bruce,x
ENTITIES   (e_{43} e_{44})]

Suppose now that the next sentence of the discourse is

93. **It** belonged to a woman **he** knew.

As it comes in, it will be labelled, say S_{93}, and assigned the syntactic parse tree

```
S NP PRO it
  AUX TENSE past
      VOICE active
  VP V belong
     PP PREP to
        NP DET ART a
           NOM N woman
              S NP PRO he
                AUX TENSE past
                    VOICE active
                VP V know
                   NP ***
           NU singular
```

(where *** is a place holder for the relative pronoun). The relative clause will be labelled $S_{93.1}$. This parse tree will then be translated into the Level-1 representation

$(Ex:\lambda(u:Woman)[Knew\ HE,u])$. Belonged IT,x

Before applying the ID-rule to identify the discourse entity associated with the existential noun phrase, this Level-1 representation will be converted into a Level-2 representation in which its pronouns are resolved (or at least a bound variable or parameterized individual interpretation ruled out).

Let us first assume HE and IT can be resolved as e_{43} (Bruce) and e_{44} (that banana) respectively, yielding the Level-2 representation

$(Ex:\lambda(u:Woman)[Knew\ PRO=e_{43},u])$. Belonged PRO=e_{44},x

(See Chapter 4, Section 2.2 for arguments why some trace of an explicit pronoun (e.g. "PRO=") should appear in the Level-2 representation.) Applying the ID-rule yields the new discourse entity

$[e_{46}$EGO ix: $\lambda(u:Woman)[Knew\ PRO=e_{43},u]x$ & Belonged PRO=e_{44},x
& **evoke** S_{93},x]

i.e., "the just-mentioned woman Bruce knew to whom that banana belonged". At this point both S_{93} and $S_{93.1}$ will be tagged with their Level-2 interpretations and their associated discourse entities (Other explicit connections can be made here as well - e.g. recording under e_{44} (the banana) the fact that it belonged to e_{46} (the woman) - i.e., Belonged e_{44},e_{46}.)

Suppose now that neither pronoun can be resolved, but that bound variable and parameterized individual interpretations can be ruled out.

(Clearly, there is nothing else from the sentence that either HE or IT can refer to.) In that case, a Level-2 representation can still be produced, with the pronouns "resolved" against unknown (but earlier evoked) individual discourse entities - i.e.,

$$(Ex:\lambda(u:Woman)[Knew\ HE=e_{?1},u])\ .\ Belonged\ IT=e_{?2},x$$

The ID-rule can then be applied to yield the following vague but still correct ID for the discourse entity evoked by the existential.

$$[e_{45} \\ EGO\quad ix:\ \lambda(u:Woman)[Knew\ HE=e_{?1},u])x\ \&\ Belonged\ IT=e_{?2},x \\ \&\ evoke\ S_{93},x]$$

i.e., "the just-mentioned woman he knew to whom it belonged".

Resolving these pronouns (both in Sentence 93 and in e_{46}'s ID) may be possible later on in the discourse. For example, one may be able to decide in parallel that (1) a subsequent pronoun refers to e_{46}, and therefore (2) the two pronouns in its ID should be resolved in particular ways. This might be the case if sentence 93 were followed by

94. Bruce remembered that the banana had been stolen from **her** Monday by a marauding monkey.

If the most likely referent for "her" is e_{46} - i.e., "the just-mentioned woman **he** know to whom **it** belonged", then world knowledge can be used to resolve both "the banana" in sentence 94 and "it" against the same discourse entity - e_{44} - and "he" against e_{43} (Bruce).

The two processes of discourse model synthesis and definite anaphor resolution are complicated by other types of anaphora, which must be resolved as well. In Chapter 4, Section 5, I will show how resolving verb phrase ellipsis fits into this scheme.

7. Summary

The main points of this chapter are the following:

1. The notion of a discourse model comprising the entities evoked or referenced in a text is useful for explicating definite anaphora (Section 1).

2. It is critical for resolving definite anaphora to be able to derive appropriate **IDs** for the discourse entities evoked by the text (Section 1).

3. The **form** of a sentence must be taken into account in deriving these **IDs** (Sections 2&5).

4. The relevant aspects of sentential form are best characterized in terms of a particular logical representation (called here a "Level-2 representation"). This can be derived from a more "surfacy" representation (a "Level-1 representation") which reflects only such aspects of meaning as were both explicit and unambiguous in its surface syntactic parse tree (Section 3).

5. The famous "donkey" sentence and others like it can be accounted for in terms of the otherwise useful notion of parameterized individuals (Section 4.3.3).

6. Discourse model synthesis and anaphor resolution are complementary processes (Section 6).

7. Other factors (tense, disjunction, negation) will also have to be taken into account if truly adequate IDs are to be formed for the discourse entities evoked by a text (Section 5).

TABLE OF CONTENTS

CHAPTER 3. "One" Anaphora

1. Introduction

In this chapter I will consider the problem of what is required for an effective treatment of "one"-anaphora. As I mentioned earlier, "one"-anaphora is my label for those terms which a speaker can substitute for a description. <*1> Sentences 1-7 illustrate some typical examples.

1a. Some cotton T-shirts are expensive
 b. but not the **one** Wendy gave Bruce yesterday.
    one = cotton T-shirt

2a. Wendy didn't give either boy a green tie-dyed T-shirt,
 b. but she gave Sue a red **one**.
    one = T-shirt or tie-dyed T-shirt

3a. I have in my cellar a '76 Beaujolais, a '71 Ch. Figeac, a '75 Durkheimer Feuerburg and a '75 Ockfener Bockstein.
 b. Shall we have the German **ones** now and the others later?
    ones = wines

4a. Wendy bought some cotton T-shirts.
 b. The largest **0** she gave to her father.
    0 = cotton T-shirt

5a. The red wines in Wendy's cellar are ready to drink.
 b. **Those** she just bought should wait a few years.
    those = the red wines

6. Red wine from Chile is usually bad, but **that** from Hungary, frequently good.
    that = red wine

7a. What is the half-life of U239?
 b. What is **it** for K40?
    it = the half-life

As can be seen from these examples, "one"-anaphora occurs in both definite and indefinite noun phrases. It is usually realized as "one", "ones" or **0** (null), but in some cases may appear as "it", "that" or "those" (see Section 5). Because a "one"-anaphor substitutes for a description, the effective procedures I shall be considering here are ones for identifying its possible antecedents.

<*1>. Notice that this is a **functional** definition: I am concerned with those things which can function as substitutes for a description. As such, the term "one"-anaphora used here subsumes such syntactically characterized phenomena as "one(s) pronominalization" and "Null NP-head anaphora" [Sag, 1976].

Now the design of effective procedures for handling "one"-anaphora requires an awareness of both the circumstances under which a speaker can felicitously use a "one"-anaphor and the reasons s/he is likely to do so. The first is a matter of the descriptions a speaker can presume a listener to be able, willing and likely to access in response to a "one"-anaphor. As with the referents of definite pronouns, these descriptions can come from three different sources - the discourse, the external environment and inference.

Considering discourse first, the language induces particular ways of viewing and describing things that **may or may not** correspond to entities in the listener's discourse model (Chapter 2, Section 1.1). For example, after sentence 2a. one would not necessarily presume any green T-shirts to be in that model, since the original sentence is a negative assertion (Chapter 2, Section 5.4). However, the existence of any referent is irrelevant to the description "tie-dyed T-shirt" being a possible antecedent for "one" in sentence 2b.

The external environment is another source of descriptions. That is, discourse entities are evoked through the discourse participants' perceptions, and these entities in turn have descriptions. How a discourse entity is described will depend upon how its corresponding perception is classified linguistically. Instances of "one"-anaphora which substitute for such descriptions have been termed "pragmatically controlled" [Hankamer and Sag, 1976]. As I mentioned above, I am calling these descriptions "non-linguistic antecedents". As well as it can be presented on paper, the following is an example of pragmatically controlled "one"-anaphora:

8. [Bonnie goes up to a balloon man at the circus and says]
   "Do you have a blue **one** with green stripes."
   one = balloon

The third source of descriptions is inference. The speaker assumes the listener can and will follow the speaker's unspoken lead to infer:

1. from description d_1 of some entity in his or her discourse model, another description d_2 of that same entity;

2. from entities $e_1,...,e_j$ with descriptions $d_1,...,d_j$ respectively, a new discourse entity e_k with description d_k.

For example, in sentence 3b. above, the listener is presumed to have classified (or be able to classify) all the discourse entities evoked by the conjoined terms in sentence 3a. as **wines**, with the latter two being German ones. The following continuation of 3a. is also possible, where a classification into white and non-white wines is presumed.

    3b'. The white **ones** will go well with tonight's dinner.

    Given these three constantly active sources of descriptions, can one be more specific about when a description can be safely accessed by a speaker via "one"-anaphora? To be accessible I believe, a description must satisfy at least two criteria. First, the listener must be directly aware of it, either because it was just mentioned in the discourse (i.e., in the same or the previous sentence) or because s/he is currently perceiving it. Secondly, if a description is not one which has been given explicitly in the discourse, the speaker must believe either that the listener can and will infer that description from descriptions given explicitly or that the listener will have described some mutual perception in the same way as the speaker.

    As to the first criterion, both speaker and listener must be able and extremely likely to conceptualize Durkheimer Feuerburg and Ockfener Bockstein as wines for either 3b. or 3b' to be used successfully.

    3a. I have in my cellar a '76 Beaujolais, a '71 Ch. Figeac, a '75
        Durkheimer Feuerberg and a '75 Ockfener Bockstein.
     b. Shall we have the German **ones** now and the others later?
     b'. The white **ones** will go well with tonight's dinner.

As to the second, suppose for example that I am visiting the Lunar Receiving Laboratory in Houston with a friend. Suppose my friend says, looking at one of the sample cases, "Only this **one** was found in the Sea of Tranquility". If my friend is a geologist, she may want to convey an antecedent description for "one" which is "medium-grained vuggy chondrite", whereas if she is just a random visitor, she may simply want to imply "rock". Notice the difference these alternate assignments make to the import of the sentence and how important it is that the speaker believe his or her way of classifying an object is shared by the listener. <*2>

<*2>. As a more mundane example, if I am holding an apple in which I've

Now as I mentioned earlier, it is important to the design of effective procedures for handling "one"-anaphora to recognize not only when a speaker can use a "one" anaphor, but also why s/he may do so. Brevity is one reason, in order to avoid repeating a long description. For example,

> 9. I promised to buy Bruce a catalogue for Sothby's upcoming wine auction, but .I haven't been able to find **one.**
> one = catalogue for Sothby's upcoming wine auction

However I think that brevity is not the most significant reason, especially when additional modifiers appear with "one". A more important reason I believe is to effect a contrast. When a speaker builds a noun phrase around a "one"-anaphor, any additional modifiers in the noun phrase can serve to differentiate and contrast the current description with some set of alternatives which the speaker perceives or believes the listener to be aware of (cf. Olson [1970]). One consequence of this is that the contrast between a restriction (R1) within the antecedent description and a restriction (R2) within the anaphor-containing noun phrase may not reflect a general antithesis (e.g. "big" vs. "little"). Rather, it may simply be a function of the current environment: where R1 holds, R2 doesn't, and vice versa. Thus in resolving a "one"-anaphor, general "either-or" axioms may not be sufficient for identifying its intended antecedent.

Moreover, not all contrasts are explicit: a modifier within a noun phrase built around a "one"-anaphor may be used to contrast with an **implicit negation** of itself within some other noun phrase. One consequence of this is that in resolving an instance of "one"-anaphora, the listener may be led to infer additional properties of a partially known entity. For example, consider the sentence

10. Of her two Dior T-shirts, Wendy prefers the yellow one.

In resolving "one" against "Dior T-shirt", the listener will be led to infer that the other of Wendy's T-shirts is not yellow.

---

just found a worm, and you come over and ask "Can I have one", what I give you (if anything) will depend on many factors, including whether I believe you have conceptualized the object as an apple, a wormy apple, a mackintosh apple, etc.

Given   then   (1) that   the   antecedent   of   "one"-anaphora   is   a
description; (2) that there are several sources for these descriptions;
(3) that   the   source   need   not   be linguistic (depending rather on the
participants' tacitly agreed-upon conceptualization of the   world);   and
(4) that   the   speaker's   motive for using "one"-anaphora is to effect a
contrast, is it possible to design procedures for identifying the
possible   antecedents   of   "one"-anaphora   and   to   incorporate   these
procedures effectively into a natural language understanding system?   In
order to   answer   these   questions,   I   first   want   to   factor   out   of
consideration   instances   of   "one"-anaphora   which   are   pragmatically
controlled, i.e. ones which depend both on the participants' immediate
non-linguistic perceptions and how entities evoked by those perceptions
are classified. <*3>   That would draw us too far away from the type of
discourse characteristic of human-computer interactions now and for some
time   to come.   I will concentrate rather on instances of "one"-anaphora
whose antecedents are more or less strongly bound to the   text.   (These
include   the   two   aforementioned cases: one, where the language induces
particular ways of describing things that may or may not   correspond   to
entities   in   the   listener's   discourse   model and the other, where the
listener augments his or her knowledge and/or beliefs about a discourse
entity with a description inferable from the given ones.)

Now if adequate procedures for identifying antecedents for this
restricted range of "one"-anaphors can be formulated, it is reasonable
to   consider   the properties a representation should possess in order to
articulate these   procedures   in   a   conceptually   clear   and   efficient
manner.   In   the next section (Section 2), I will discuss what at least
some of these properties are. All together they seem to   argue   that   a
reasonable source of candidate antecedents for "one"-anaphora would be a
representation   which   captures   certain aspects of sentence meaning but
remains very close to the surface word order and syntax.   Two possible
representations - syntactic   surface   structure   and   the   Level-2   logical
representation introduced in Chapter 2, Section 3 - are discussed in

---

<*3>. Those readers concerned with pragmatically controlled anaphora
may find relevant the discussion in Section 6 on how people classify
"named" (rather than "described") entities.

Section 3, with some arguments given in favor of the latter. This is followed in Section 4 by an example of its use in identifying candidates. In Section 5, I will take up differences between the various representatives of "one"-anaphora - i.e., "one", "ones", 0, "that", "those" and "it". Finally in Section 6, I will consider some types of non-explicit descriptions which can also serve as antecedents for "one"-anaphora. These latter point out the importance to successful communication via "one"-anaphora of culturally shared ways of reacting to language and conceptualizing the external world.

2. Requirements on a Representation

2.1 Preserving Noun Phrases as Structural Units

First, since the antecedents of "one"-anaphora are descriptions, an appropriate representation would be one that allows descriptions to stand out clearly: no kind of homogeneous representation of a sentence's meaning would be appropriate. To illustrate this, consider again example 1.

    1a. Some cotton T-shirts are expensive,
     b. but not the **one** that Wendy gave Bruce yesterday.

In a "flat" predicate calculus type of representation (ignoring here the distinction between "some" plural and "some" singular, sentence 1a. might be represented as

    (Ex). Cotton x & T-shirt x & Expensive x

Now intuitively, the antecedent of "one" in sentence 1b. is something like "cotton T-shirt", but from the flat predicate calculus representation, there is no more reason to suppose that Cotton and T-shirt form a possible antecedent than Cotton and Expensive, or T-shirt and Expensive, or any one or all three. That is, there is no **structural** indication that the description "Cotton T-shirt" is a referenceable unit, while "Expensive T-shirt" and "Expensive Cotton (thing)" are not.

The same point about referenceable units can be made about **non-referential** noun phrases (predicate nominatives). For example,

    11a. Dr. Bert is an excellent dentist.
      b. Dr. Bruce is a terrible **one**.

12a. Dr. Bert is an excellent dentist,
  b. and another **one** I know lives down the block.

The descriptions which serve as antecedents to these two examples of
"one"-anaphora both come from the non-referential noun phrases in the a.
sentences. <*4>   As I mentioned earlier, a noun phrase containing a
"one" anaphor can itself be used either referentially (as in sentence
12b.) or non-referentially (sentence 11b.), independent of the source of
"one"'s antecedent.

   The upshot of this is that a representation for English text can
facilitate finding linguistically evoked antecedents for "one"-anaphora
only if all noun phrases, regardless of function, are preserved as
structural units.

2.2 Further Factoring of Descriptions

   A second requirement on an adequate representation for identifying
possible antecedents for "one"-anaphora is that the head noun of the
noun phrase, which conveys the principal attribute of the description,
must be distinguished from the remainder of the noun phrase (i.e.
adjectives, noun-noun modifiers, prepositional phrases and relative
clauses) which convey restrictions on that attribute. The reason for
this can be seen in the following example.

   13. Wendy bought a tie-dyed cotton T-shirt and Fred bought an
       embroidered **one.**

Whether intuitively "one" substitutes for the description "cotton
T-shirt" or "tie-dyed cotton T-shirt" or merely "T-shirt", the primary
class denoted by the noun phrase - that is, "T-shirt" - must be part of
that description. It seems to be a fact of English that the only
descriptions accessible to "one"-anaphora are ones which include the
head noun from a noun phrase. Thus it is important to distinguish the
head noun, in order for a representation to be adequate for
"one"-anaphora.

<*4>. A non-referential noun phrase is one that does not evoke a
discourse entity. If Sentence 11a. above were followed by a sentence
·like "I get cavities just to see him", "him" could only refer to "Dr.
Bert" and not to "the excellent dentist mentioned in sentence 11a." For
more on non-referential noun phrases, see [Kuno, 1970].

Another important point to recognize is that this factoring of descriptions should be represented in a very "surfacy" manner. That is, no attempt should be made to replace the (surface) concepts explicitly mentioned with their definitions in terms of more primitive concepts. To do so I believe would cause problems in identifying candidate antecedents for other types of anaphora -- missing verb phrases for example. If a phrase like "bottle opener" were represented in the same way as the semantically more explicit "device designed to open bottles", then the predicates corresponding to "be designed to open bottles" and "open bottles" would incorrectly be available as candidate antecedents for a missing verb phrase and "device" would be available for "one"anaphora. Of course, if a sentence explicitly contains the phrase "designed to open bottles", then the above predicates must be so available, e.g.

    14. I thought this plastic monkey was designed to open bottles,
       ...but it wasn't **0**.
       0 = designed to open bottles
       ...but it doesn't **0**.
       0 = open bottles

This is basically an argument for the relevance of "surfacy" representations to identifying candidate antecedents for anaphoric expressions. It should not be taken as denying the value of semantically "deeper" representations for, say, choosing among possible candidates. For example, one must certainly identify the underlying relationship between "cotton" and "T-shirt" in the phrase "cotton T-shirt", if one is to accept the description "cotton T-shirt" as a possible antecedent for "one" in the phrase "one made by Cardin" and reject it as a possible antecedent for "one" in the phrase "one made of rayon".

2.3 Disambiguating Word Senses

Even though an explicit lexical item should not be replaced with its definition in terms of more primitive concepts if a representation is to be adequate for handling "one"-anaphora, it does seem that a semantically ambiguous lexical item should be replaced by a token indicating its recognized sense. This holds with the notion that the main function of "one"-anaphora is to effect a contrast between the current description (built around the "one"-anaphor) and some set of alternatives the speaker believes the listener to be aware of. For most things, such alternatives suggest themselves more readily in response to a sense association than to one based on sound similarities alone (i.e., "surface ear" effects). The exception seems to be pronouns, as I shall discuss in the next section.

However, this is not to say that sound alone can **never** justify a speaker's use of "one"-anaphora: frequently in word play, it is only sound similarity that the speaker uses for justification. For example, the following sentences are either "creative" or "bizarre", depending on whether or not one accepts this "sound" justification.

15. Wendy could wear the taffeta shift to the dance because her
    sister worked the late-night **one** at the plant.
    one = shift <*5>

16. My brother thinks both rhododendron plants and chemical ones
    pollute the atmosphere.
    one = plant

17. My brother hates balls thrown by society ladies and also **ones**
    thrown by rival pitchers.
    one = ball

For me these sentences exemplify a type of word play, very similar to **zeugma**, which is the name given to situations where one word governs several others, each in a different way, e.g. "Bruce takes sugar in his coffee, pride in his work and offense at the slightest innuendo."

As to the implications of this for handling "one"-anaphora, if a single representation is required to serve as a source of antecedents for all instances of "one"-anaphora, then back pointers should be provided from the sense tokens used in the representation to the lexical items on the surface. (These can be as simple as the implicit pointer to the word "ball" contained in a token like "ball$_1$".

<*5>. One sense of "shift" denotes a type of dress, usually straight or A-line.

2.4 Resolving Definite Pronouns

A fourth requirement on a representation adequate for handling "one"-anaphora - the last one I am currently aware of - is that descriptions arising from noun phrases containing definite pronouns must be accessible as antecedents in **both** their resolved and their unresolved forms. To see that this is so, consider the following example.

18. The doctor compared Bruce's Freudian analysis of his mother with Wendy's Reichian **one**.

If the referent of "he" (i.e., "his") in example 18 is Bruce, there seem to be two possible antecedents for "one" --

(i) analysis of his (Bruce's) mother

(ii) analysis of her (own) mother.

If the referent of "his" is not Bruce, but rather someone else - say, the doctor - then there seems to be only one possible antecedent for "one", namely

(iii) analysis of his (the doctor's) mother

As for deciding which reading is preferable, that may require as much world knowledge as resolving a definite pronoun. While (i) seems to me the best reading for sentence 18 above, in examples like the following, the description containing the **unresolved** pronoun seems to be the only antecedent that suggests itself beside the head noun alone.

19. Wendy will pay up to 70 dollars for a dress she can wear off the rack, but Sally won't pay more than fifty for **one**.
    one = a dress she (Sally) can wear without altering
        ≠ a dress she (Wendy) can wear without altering

20. Bruce gave Sally a coat they both liked and Fred gave Wendy **one** too.
    one ≠ coat they (Bruce and Sally) both liked
        = coat they (Fred and Wendy) both liked
        = coat

This seems to me a matter of pragmatics - i.e., women usually buy dresses off the rack for themselves. But insofar as it impinges on the task of identifying possible antecedents for "one"-anaphora, it would seem that both forms of a description must be accessible: the form in which the pronoun is explicitly there (as on the surface) and the form in which it has been resolved.

3. Possible Representations

What kind of representation for the incoming discourse would satisfy the requirements set out in Section 2 and serve as a rich, if somewhat incomplete, source of antecedents for "one"-anaphora?

3.1 Syntactic Surface Structure

One representation that suggests itself is a syntactic surface-structure parse tree. Syntactic surface-structure seems to satisfy at least two of the above requirements: all noun phrases, whether referential or not, are distinct structural units, and within a noun phrase, the head noun is usually separate from those parts denoting restrictions. However, the kind of parse tree I see being produced initially (cf. Chapter 2, Section 6) would not be sufficient, since neither word senses nor pronoun references are presumed to be resolved. <*6> It is conceivable that the initial parse tree could be annotated with this information after its appropriate Level-2 semantic interpretation had been produced. If so, it would probably be an reasonable arena for identifying candidate antecedents for "one"-anaphor whose source was the explicit discourse. (If one chose this approach, then one would probably attempt to rely on syntactic and phonological cues as guides in one's search for candidates and then to use semantic and pragmatic information to judge their suitability.)

3.2 Level-2 Interpretations

Another possible sentence representation to search for candidate antecedents for "one"-anaphora is the Level-2 semantic interpretation introduced in Chapter 2, Section 3. One advantage of this representation is, as I just mentioned, that its role in discourse model construction and anaphor resolution in most cases requires word senses and pronouns to have been resolved (cf. Chapter 2, Section 6). On the other hand, one disadvantage is that it is further away from the surface, making it more difficult to notice and make use of cues based

---

<*6>. This initial parse tree is presumed to be produced based on purely syntactic criteria. In general, this is not sufficient to resolve word sense or pronoun reference ambiguities.

on sound similarity. What I shall do in the remainder of this section is to show how a Level-2 interpretation is justified as a source of candidate antecedents for "one"-anaphora.

I mentioned in Section 2.1 that a representation can help in identifying antecedents for "one"-anaphora only if it preserves noun phrases as structural units. The Level-2 interpretation does so through the use of restricted quantifiers and definite descriptions. Recall that in a restricted quantifier, the quantification operator (e.g. ∀, E), its variable of quantification and the class that it ranges over (noted implicitly as a predicate) constitute a structural unit of the form (Qx:P) where Q is a quantification operator and P, a predicate. Similarly definite descriptions constitute structural units of the form $ix:S_x$, where S_x is an open sentence free in x. For example, "The boy is happy" can be represented as

Happy ix:Boy x

and "The boys are happy" as

Happy ix:**maxset**(Boy)x

Recall that both P and S_x can become arbitrarily complex, through the use of the abstraction operator and Boolean connectives. Thus even noun phrases containing relative clauses and/or other modifiers will appear as structural units (cf. Chapter 2, Section 3.1). (Predicate nominatives, e.g. "a good doctor" in "Bruce is a good doctor", must also be represented as structural units. These I will get to shortly.)

Another requirement on representations suitable for handling "one"-anaphora was that the head noun, denoting the primary property of the description, be kept separate from those parts denoting restrictions on that property. This is why descriptions in the Level-1 and Level-2 representations have the form

<P>   or $\lambda(<var>:<P>)[S_{<var>}]$

where <P> is a predicate, <var> is a variable and $S_{<var>}$ is an open sentence free in <var>. Alone <P> is shorthand for $\lambda(<var>:<P>)[True]$.

For example, one can represent

"T-shirt"   as T-shirt

"cotton T-shirt"   as λ(u:T-shirt)[Cotton u]

"T-shirt that Wendy gave Fred"   as λ(u:T-shirt)[Gave Wendy,Fred,u]

(As mentioned above, the first is merely a shorthand for λ(u:T-shirt)[True].)

The semantics of these descriptions will depend on whether or not they can be evaluated independently. For predicates which can be evaluated independently, this means

($\forall$x: λ(u:P)[Qu]) . Rx   :=:   ($\forall$x) . [Px & Qx] ==> Rx

(Ex: λ(u:P)[Qu]) . Rx   :=:   (Ex) . Px & Qx & Rx

and informally, for definite descriptions,

R ix: λ(u:P)[Qu]x   :=:
      (Ex) . Px & Qx & Rx & "x is the only P currently in
            focus such that Q"

where the quoted phrase is meant to stand for some indication of context-dependent uniqueness. Predicates which cannot be evaluated independently <*7> will have a more complex semantics, such as the intensional semantics presented in Montague [1974]. (In Montague's intensional semantics, the extensional evaluation presented above for complex predicates is merely a special case.) What is important to recognize is that this feature of the Level-2 representation - i.e., that the predicate associated with the head noun of the noun phrase is structurally distinct - does not interfere with the assignment of an appropriate truth-value semantics.

As for predicate nominatives, we can again use the abstraction operator to create the descriptions they assert of their subject noun phrases. For example,

21. Bert is an excellent dentist.
    Bert, λ(u:Dentist)[Excellent u]

(In the notation I am using, a simple predicate name will precede its arguments, as in Love Bruce,Wendy. For clarity however, a complex predicate will follow its subject as in the above example.) I would

---

<*7>. "Large" is such a predicate. "A large banana" should not be interpreted as an object which is large and which is a banana. Rather it is an object which is large with respect to being a banana.

then claim that the structural units of Q-restrictions, definite descriptions and predicate nominative descriptions are the sources of candidate antecedents for "one"-anaphora, in those cases where they intuitively seem to derive from the text.

4. Identifying Candidate Antecedents

The following example will illustrate using the Level-2 interpretation of a sentence to identify linguistically evoked candidate antecedents for "one"-anaphora:

22a. Wendy gave each boy a green T-shirt.
  b. She gave Sue a red one.

Looking first at sentence 22a, its Level-2 interpretation can be written

(i) $(\forall x:Boy)(Ey:\lambda(u:T\text{-}shirt)[Green\ u])$. Gave Wendy,x,y

Looking next at sentence 22b, its Level-1 representation (i.e., the one in which, **inter alia**, anaphoric and elliptic expressions have not yet been resolved) can be written as

(ii) $(Ez:\lambda(u:P?)[Red\ u])$. Gave SHE, Sue, z

where P? stands for the currently unknown predicate associated with z. In other words, there is something of unknown type P? that should be derivable from context, which we are told is red, which some known female SHE gave Sue. Assuming that the discourse entity associated with Wendy is the most plausible referent for SHE, the task is to identify possible antecedents for P?

I will consider as possible antecedents for P? all "recently" mentioned definite descriptions, predicate descriptions and Q-restrictions, independent of their particular quantifiers. ("Recent" seems to mean here the current sentence, the previous one, and perhaps the one before that. It does not seem to be affected by task structure [Grosz, 1977] or story structure, or any of the other factors that seem to change the set of available antecedents for definite pronouns like "he", "it", etc.)

The Q-restrictions explicitly given in (i) are Boy, T-shirt and $\lambda(u:T\text{-}shirt)[Green\ u]$. Notice that when one restriction is constructed out of other ones via the abstraction operator, all of them can be included as candidate antecedents for P?. Deciding which candidate antecedent is the most plausible seems to me a task for a reasoning procedure which has a knowledge of both the world and the specific situation. As such, it is beyond the scope of this thesis. However, I might say that in this case, such a reasoner would have to consider the need to be able to predicate Red of an entity of type P?. This would eliminate λ(u:T-shirt)[Green u] through application of something like a "clashing-color" axiom: if something is green, it is not red. (Notice that if sentence 22b. had been

22b. Fred, she gave an extra-large one.

there would be no **semantic** reason to eliminate this description as a plausible antecedent unless it was a fact of the domain that extra-large T-shirts could not be green.) Such a reasoner might also take into account "stylistics" in the form of structural parallelism, to argue for plausibility. That is, if two successive sentences are structurally similar ("parallel") and in the latter, anaphoric "one" helps to fill role R (here, the object), then it has a very plausible antecedent in the noun phrase filling role R in the previous sentence (here, the previous object "a green T-shirt").

However, my objective in this chapter is not to specify procedures for choosing among candidate antecedents; it is rather to define the realms in which such candidates may be found and consider the machinery (including an appropriately structured representation language) which would facilitate their identification.

There are two major gaps in the above presentation: first, it seems to assume that the listener can assign an unambiguous interpretation to a noun phrase in terms of class restrictions, and secondly, it assumes that additional modifiers in the "one"-anaphor noun phrase modify the antecedent description as a whole rather than just some part of it. The latter assumption implies that the following sequence would be anomalous

23. While I like lime green T-shirts, Wendy prefers forest **ones.**

(where both "lime" and "forest" are intended to modify "green" to yield particular color names, and "one" substitutes for the non-constituent

"green T-shirt"). I think this latter assumption is basically valid
since, returning to the notion of "contrast", it implies that a speaker
is more likely to effect a contrast around some **property** (or set of
properties) that all the contrasted items possess than a contrast around
some random string.

As to the first point, it is obviously not always the case that a
listener can assign an unambiguous interpretation to a noun phrase in
terms of class restrictions. For example, the phrase "a green cotton
T-shirt" may be understood as a **green** <*8> cotton T-shirt (i.e., a
cotton T-shirt whose color was green), a **green cotton** T-shirt (i.e., a
T-shirt made of green cotton), or perhaps even as a green **cotton** T-shirt
(i.e., a green T-shirt made of cotton). These differences would be
reflected in how these phrases are represented in terms of restricted
classes:

   (i) $\lambda(r:\lambda(s:T\text{-}shirt)[Cotton\ s])[Green\ r]$
  (ii) $\lambda(r:T\text{-}shirt)[\lambda(s:Cotton)[Green\ s]\ r]$
 (iii) $\lambda(r:\lambda(s:T\text{-}shirt)[Green\ s])[Cotton\ r]$

They would thus also result in different constituent descriptions being
available as candidate antecedents for "one"-anaphora. For example,
assuming (i) is the correct interpretation of "green cotton T-shirt",
the candidate antecedents for "one" in "a rayon one" would include only

   T-shirt   "T-shirt"

  $\lambda(s:T\text{-}shirt)[Cotton\ s]$ "Cotton T-shirt"

  $\lambda(r:\lambda(s:T\text{-}shirt)[Cotton\ s])[Green\ r]$ "green cotton T-shirt"

If cotton and rayon are presumed to be contrastive, then the only
truly plausible antecedent for "one" in "a rayon one" is T-shirt. On
the other hand, assuming (iii) is the correct interpretation, the
candidate antecedents for "one" would include

   T-shirt   "T-shirt"

  $\lambda(s:T\text{-}shirt)[Green\ s]$ "green T-shirt"

  $\lambda(r:\lambda(s:T\text{-}shirt)[Green\ s])[Cotton\ r]$ "green cotton T-shirt

Now even though the latter would presumably also be dismissible on the
rayon/cotton contrast, two candidate antecedents would still remain:

<*8>. Underlining is meant to indicate heavy stress.

T-shirt, as above, and "green T-shirt". If Bruce bought a green cotton T-shirt and Wendy bought a rayon one, then it is possible on only this interpretation for the listener to assume she bought a green rayon T-shirt. Of course, on any interpretation, the listener would not be wrong in assuming she bought a rayon T-shirt.

My point is that except in cases where a speaker uses heavy stress, altered speech rate, etc. to convey his or her own sense of a noun phrase, a listener may have no way of deriving that sense unambiguously. In the case of text, where stress offers no cue, the difficulty of this task is increased. Holding all possible interpretations around is not an attractive solution.

One possible though extremely conservative response to this problem is an "all-or-nothing" approach. According to this approach, only **two** kinds of descriptions are considered as candidate antecedents for "one"-anaphora: the **complete** description associated with a noun phrase and the description associated with just the head noun. The former guarantees a correct response in situations like

    24a. Wendy gave each of her brothers a green cotton T-shirt.
      b. The **one** she gave to Fred didn't fit.
         one = green cotton T-shirt

    25a. Wendy likes green cotton T-shirts.
      b. She frequently wears a bespangled **one** she bought at DR.
         one = green cotton T-shirt

(provided in 24b. that Fred is one of Wendy's brothers). A characteristic of such situations seems to be that additional modifiers in the anaphor-containing noun phrase are used by the speaker to distinguish among members of some previously established class. In example 24b, it is the class of green cotton T-shirts each of which Wendy gave to one of her brothers (cf. Chapter 2, Section 4.3.1), and in example 25b, it is the class of green cotton T-shirts.

Choosing only the head noun descriptions on the other hand guarantees at least a partially correct response in most other situations, e.g.

    26a. Wendy gave each of her brothers a green T-shirt from DR.
      b. The **one** she gave her sister was even more expensive.

27a. Wendy likes green cotton T-shirts,
    b. but she frequently wears a bespangled **one** she bought at DR.
Here, whatever else may be true of the referents of the "one"-anaphor noun phrases, it is nevertheless true that they are T-shirts. <*9>

    A consequence of this conservative approach is that at the level of representation used to **suggest** linguistically evoked candidate antecedents for "one"-anaphora, the only necessary structure within a definite description, Q-restriction or predicate nominative is one which separates the head noun from additional restrictions (except in the special case noted above). It is not necessary to decide how the entire description conveyed by the noun phrase has been constructed from its constituents. However, since the choice of an entire description as the most plausible antecedent may depend upon knowing its compatibility with modifiers in the "one"-anaphor noun phrase, this may force a commitment to one or another more highly structured description. So again we have a case where the resolution of an earlier ambiguity or vagueness comes about through the current need to resolve an anaphoric expression.

5. Representatives of 'One'-Anaphora

    As I mentioned earlier, "one"-anaphora can be instantiated in several different ways - "one", "ones", "that", "those", "it" and **0**. Here I shall begin to characterize each of these with respect to when and where it can occur. My purpose is to help wherever possible in recognizing where something is functioning as a "one"-anaphor as opposed to a definite pronoun, a deictic pronoun or determiner, or even as a cardinal number. (I do not claim completeness for what follows - just that it is a useful start.)

<*9>. This conservative approach fails in just those cases where something described as an "<A><B>" is not a <B> at all. For example, a toy camel is not a camel.

    (i) Bruce was playing with the toy camel his mother had given him
        and Wendy was playing with the **one** she had bought herself.

Here postulating only "camel" and "toy camel that his (Bruce's) mother had given him (Bruce)" as possible antecedents for "one" in sentence (i) will lead in either case to an incorrect response.

5.1 That and Those

"That" and "those" have a built-in definite determiner: they are equivalent to "the one(s)". A noun phrase headed by "one(s)" on the other hand will be definite or indefinite depending on its quantifier or determiner: "one", "seven blue ones" and "some red ones" are indefinite noun phrases (i.e. they evoke new instances of the entities they describe), while "the seven blue ones" and "that one with the red stripes" are definite (i.e. they refer to existing entities in the surrounding context).

"That" and "those" are representatives of "one" anaphora, rather than being deictic pronouns or determiners, when they occur in the following context

$$NP ::= \begin{cases} \text{that} \\ \text{those} \end{cases} + <\text{postmod}>^+$$

where <postmod> stands for noun phrase post-modifiers like prepositional phrases, relative clauses, adjectival phrases, etc., and the superscript (Kleene) plus (+) indicates one or more instances of them. Where there is no post-modifier, "that" and "those" are deictic pronouns - definite pronouns which are resolvable against something in the shared spatio-temporal or linguistic context of the speaker (writer) and the listener (reader), e.g. "Wendy bought those at Filene's". Where there is an explicit head (possibly with other modifiers), "that" and "those" are functioning as deictic determiners. Note that in this latter case, the head of the noun phrase may very well be "one(s)"! For example,

28. I want those green ones with blue stripes.

5.2 0

When a "one"-anaphor replaces the description of a mass concept, it may be instantiated as null (**0**), provided there are no post-modifiers. If there are, then "that" or "it" must be used. For example,

29. Bruce prefers red wine to white **0**.
    0 = wine

30. Bruce prefers Hungarian wine to (**that**, ***0**) from Chile.
    that = wine

Where a "one"-anaphor is realized as 0, the problem may be one of
recognizing that anything is missing. For example, in the sentence

    31. Bruce prefers red to white, although green is his favorite
        color.

"red" may either refer to the color in the abstract or be short for "red
wines", as in the example above.

A "one"-anaphor may also (but not necessarily) be realized as 0 in
the following syntactic context

$$\text{NP} ::= (\langle\text{art}\rangle) \begin{Bmatrix} \langle\text{possessive}\rangle \\ \langle\text{superlative}\rangle \\ \langle\text{ordinal}\rangle \end{Bmatrix} 0 \ + \ \langle\text{postmod}\rangle^{*}$$

that is, in the context of an optional definite article, either a
possessive, a superlative or an ordinal, followed by any number of
post-modifiers, including none. <*10>   For example,

    32. Although Bruce ate seven cream-filled brownies, the last 0 was
        eaten by Fred.
        0 = cream-filled brownie

    33. Bruce caught several hairy spiders today. The largest 0 that he
        found measured four inches across.
        0 = hairy spider

5.3 It

Since "it" as a definite pronoun has the widest range of possible
referents (cf. Chapter 1, Section 4), there is a definite advantage to
separating out at least those instances of "it" as a representative of
"one"-anaphora.   Basically,   "it"   can   substitute   for a unique
description, as distinct from one which could possibly hold of several
entities.   (In the latter case, "one" or "ones" would be appropriate.)
For example,

    34a. Carter is the president of the United States.
      b. He became it when Ford was defeated for re-election.
        it = the president of the United States

Here "it", in predicate nominative position, clearly does not have a
referent: its sole function is to substitute for a unique description.

<*10>. Adjectives and/or noun-noun modifiers may also occur in this
context if the antecedent of the "one"-anaphor is a mass term, cf.
sentences 29-30 above.

In other positions in which it functions in this way, whether it **also** has a referent is a separate issue. (Several linguists [Hintikka & Carlson 1977; Geach 1962; Karttunen 1969; Partee 1972] have discussed what I believe to be similar (although not necessarily the same) cases of "it" under the label "pronouns of laziness". For example

  35. The man who gives his paycheck to his wife is wiser than the man who gives **it** to his mistress. [Karttunen, 1969]
      it = his paycheck

Notice that if "it" were taken as a definite anaphor referring to a previously evoked discourse entity, the ID-rule given in Chapter 2 would only provide as possible referents

  e_1 - "the man who gives his paycheck to his wife"

  e_2 - "e_1's wife"

Thus I believe that seeing these as examples of "one"-anaphora instantiated by "it", instead of examples of "it" as a definite pronoun, can simplify any theory to be proposed for definite pronouns.)

One syntactic context where it is relatively easy to identify "it" as a representative of "one"-anaphora is where "it" is followed by one or more post-modifiers, e.g.

  36a. What is the voltage drop across R6?
   b. What is **it** across R7?
      it = the voltage drop

  37a. Give me the overall concentration of FeO in each breccia.
   b. What is **it** for Fe_3O_4?
      it = the overall concentration in each breccia

6. Non-explicit Descriptions

Up to now I have been primarily discussing candidate antecedents for "one"-anaphora which come "free" (in some sense) from the discourse. In this final section of the chapter, I want to discuss other sorts of descriptions which are accessible to "one"-anaphora as well.

First, a caveat. I do not believe it possible to limit **a priori** (1) exactly the way a speaker will conceptualize aspects of a discourse or the outside world, (2) the assumptions he or she will make about those conceptualizations being shared by the listener and thus (3) how freely he or she will use "one"-anaphora to access non-explicit but presumed shared descriptions. However, I do feel that there are certain types of inferences which are acceptable as sources of non-explicit descriptions, which people sometimes assume and which might be incorporated into a practical system for generating candidate antecedents for "one"-anaphora. These are the ones I feel are most appropriate to discuss in this final section of the chapter.

The first type of inference seems to be not very productive, though it is interesting from a theoretical point of view. It has been discussed under the name "anaphoric islands" first by Postal [1969] and later by Bresnan [1971] and others. This type of inference is based solely on morphological and phonological similarity. It derives from an explicit description a modified form which serves as the antecedent for a "one"-anaphor, e.g.

    38a. Bruce's face was mirrored across the room. It upset him so much
         that he broke a particularly valuable one.
         one = mirror

      b. Bruce wanted to become a great violinist, so he bought an old
         one that was claimed to be a Strad.
         one = violin

      c. Max knifed me before I even realized he had **one**.
         one = (a) knife

These derivations are based both on the **form** of the explicit description as well as on its **sense**. Notice also that slight variations which disturb this morphological/phonological similarity seem to destroy the possibility of an anaphor-antecedent relationship, for example

    39a. Bruce's face was reflected across the room. It upset him so
         much that he broke **one**.
         one = ?

      b. Bruce wanted to become a great flautist, so he bought **one** that
         was claimed to belong to Rampal.
         one = ?

      c. Max stabbed me before I even realized he had **one**.
         one = ?

Thirdly, notice that the antecedent of the "one"-anaphor must be both a morphological and phonological sub-piece of the explicit description that suggested it. The listener cannot be expected to identify the antecedent of a "one" anaphor, if it is morphologically and

phonologically **more** complex (in some unknown way) than material given
explicitly, e.g.

    40a.*Bruce bought a violin because he wanted to become a great **one**.
       one = violinist

      b.*Begin wherever your story has a logical **one**.
       one = beginning

Moreover, when there is an explicit description (Q-restriction or
predicate nominative) around that would make a **plausible** antecedent, it
does not appear to be the case that a non-explicit description would
ever be the **correct** one. For example

    41. Max knifed me with his stiletto before I even realized he had
       one.

Since "stiletto" is a plausible antecedent for "one", it is
inconceivable that the author of this sentence intended it to stand
merely for the superordinate class, "knife".

Given these constraints on the distribution of this class of
antecedents for "one"-anaphora (and there are perhaps more), it would
seem possible to annotate one's lexicon once and for all with all the
possible cases. Moreover, if one handles words like "violinist" through
a process of derivational morphology rather than as separate entities in
the lexicon, the embedded morphologically and phonologically similar
words like "violin" would seem to come free. As to accessing this
lexical information, it is probably the case that one would not want to
do so unless no plausible antecedent for "one" could be found by other
means.

Non-explicit candidate antecedents for "one"-anaphora also seem to
be available from the IDs of discourse entities evoked by existential
quantifiers (cf. Chapter 2, Section 4). These are descriptions of the
form "an A which P's" which come from assertions like "An A Ps", "Some
A's P", etc. For example,

    42a. Some cotton T-shirts are expensive.
      b. Wendy gave (a black) **one** to Bruce just yesterday.

    43a. Wendy gave Fred some cotton T-shirts.
      b. Her friend Sue liked the red **ones**.

    44a. Wendy gave Fred some cotton T-shirts.
      b. The first 0 was too large, but the remaining **ones** fit.

45a. Each boy gave Wendy a cotton T-shirt.
   b. The red **ones** she found too gaudy.

For some people, the most plausible antecedents for these five instances
of "one"-anaphora (i.e. either "one" or 0) are "expensive cotton
T-shirt" in example 42b., "cotton T-shirts that Wendy gave Fred" in
examples 43b. and 44b, and "cotton T-shirts, each of which some boy gave
Wendy" in example 45b. Other interpretations like "cotton T-shirt" and
"T-shirt" are possible, but less likely. Notice that these are just the
IDs of the discourse entities evoked by the existentially quantified
noun phrases, cf.

46a. Some cotton T-shirts are expensive.
   b. **They** have designer labels and cost twenty dollars apiece.

47a. Wendy gave Fred some cotton T-shirts.
   b. **They** fit him perfectly.

In sentence 46b., the referent of "they" is the discourse entity
describable as "the just-mentioned expensive cotton T-shirts" and in
sentence 47b., it is the entity describable as "the just-mentioned
cotton T-shirts which Wendy gave Fred.

Notice that with similar sentences which do not evoke new entities
into the listener's discourse model, this additional description does
not present itself as a possible antecedent for "one".

48a. No cotton T-shirts are expensive.
   b. Wendy gave (a black) one to Bruce just yesterday.
      one = T-shirt, cotton T-shirt, *expensive cotton T-shirt

49a. Wendy didn't give Fred a cotton T-shirt,
   b. even though her friend Sue liked the red **ones**.
      ones = T-shirts, cotton T-shirts,
             *cotton T-shirts that Wendy didn't give Fred

In these cases, only "cotton T-shirt" and "T-shirt" are held to be
possible antecedents for "one", since these sentences, unlike 42-45, do
not evoke new T-shirt entities into the listener's model. <*11>   Given
that the system I am envisioning computes an appropriate ID for every
new discourse entity (or if there is an ambiguity, the set of

---

<*11>. As I mentioned in Chapter 2, Section 5.4, the issue of negation
and the evocation of discourse entities is a complex one. However, it
does seem to be the case that only the explicit descriptions "T-shirt"
and "cotton T-shirt" are available for "one"-anaphora in this case, no
matter what is more specifically being negated.

alternatively possible **IDs**), it should be simple to make them available
as antecedents for "one"-anaphora as well.

There is an alternative way of viewing the phenomena illustrated in
sentences 42-45 which does not involve expanding the search space of
possible candidates to include descriptions of newly evoked entities.
According to this method, only the explicit descriptions "T-shirt" and
"cotton T-shirt" are made available as candidate antecedents for
"one"-anaphora. Looking first at examples 43b, 44b and 45b, after
resolving **0** and "one" against either "T-shirt" or "cotton T-shirt", the
system attempts to identify whether or not the resulting definite
description - i.e., "the red (cotton) T-shirts" and "the first (cotton)
T-shirt" - are themselves anaphoric. It should find that these noun
phrases refer to the red T-shirts that Wendy gave Fred (sentence 43b.),
the first of the recently mentioned cotton T-shirts that Wendy gave Fred
(sentence 44b.), the remaining cotton T-shirts that Wendy gave Fred
(sentence 44b.) and the red T-shirts belonging to the set of T-shirts,
each of which some boy gave Wendy (sentence 45b.).

In processing example 42b, "one" would first be resolved against
either "cotton T-shirt" or "T-shirt". Then **the same plausible inference**
<**12> that would promote "expensive cotton T-shirt" as the most
plausible antecedent for "one" under the first solution method could be
used to suggest that the black (cotton) T-shirt which Wendy gave Bruce
just yesterday was expensive. (That is, why remark on cotton T-shirts
being expensive without meaning to imply that of the next-mentioned one
that Wendy gave Bruce?)

The problem with this solution method is that it places particular
requirements on the determiner of the "one"-anaphor noun phrase, while
the first, "discourse entity" method does not. For example,

50a. Wendy gave Fred some cotton T-shirts.
  . b. Her friend Sue liked a red **one**.

By the first method, "cotton T-shirt which Wendy gave Fred" is a
plausible antecedent for "one". However by the second method, there is

---

<**12>. probably one that makes use of Grice's relevancy principle
[Grice, 1975]

no reason to want to go further than "a cotton T-shirt" or "a T-shirt",
since the phrase "a red (cotton) T-shirt" is not anaphoric, while "the
red (cotton) T-shirt" is.

The final type of inference which I will mention seems a much more
marginal source of non-explicit antecedents for "one"-anaphora than the
previous two. (In fact, I am still finding it difficult to characterize
it, although it seems associated with whether or not - or to what degree
- people impose some superordinate classification on a set of things
they are presented with.) Consider the following examples, the first of
which is repeated from the introductory examples. <*13>

    3a. I have in my cellar a '76 Beaujolais, a '71 Chateau Figeac, a
        '75 Durkheimer Feuerburg and a '75 Ockfener Bockstein.
     b. Shall we drink the German **ones** now and the others later?

    51a. I have in my cellar a '76 Beaujolais, a '71 Chateau Figeac, a
        '75 Durkheimer Feuerburg and a '75 Ockfener Bockstein.
     b. Shall we drink the oldest **one** first?
        one = wine

    52a. Compare Dahomy, Gabon, Cameroon, Nigeria and Tanzania.
     b. Only the **ones** on the coast have a subsistence economy.
        one =? (African) country

    53a. Compare Dahomey, Gabon, Cameroon, Nigeria and Tanzania with the
        rest of Africa.
     b. Only **ones** on the coast have a subsistence economy.
        one =? (African) country

    54a. I know about Advent, Bose, AR and KLH,
     b. but about Japanese **ones**, you'll have to ask Fred.
        one =? speaker, speaker producer, ...?

What these examples seem to involve is the speaker's (1) turning an
explicit set description (i.e. the presented list of objects) into an
implicit description (i.e. one based on a defining property); (2) using
that inferred description as an antecedent for "one"-anaphora; and
(3) presuming the listener's ability and willingness to do the same.

There are a few things to note here. First the examples in which
"one" occurs in a definite noun phrase (Examples 3, 51 and 52) seem to
be simpler to process than the ones in which it occurs in an indefinite

---

<*13>. Where an example sounds strange, it may be because of the
feeling that the antecedent of "one" must be something that occurred in
a previous sentence that isn't shown here.

noun phrase. This may be because, from a practical point of view, it is not necessary to find an antecedent for "one" in the definite case. Since in going from a Level-1 to a Level-2 representation of a sentence, each definite description is considered as a possible anaphor, if it is one, the modifiers explicitly given in the description may be sufficient to determine its referent without having to resolve "one". However, this will not work in the indefinite cases, which **will** require an ability to collect up some set of individuals and infer an appropriate set description. This may be why the indefinite cases seem marginal or difficult to process.

Notice that all the examples I gave above involved a list of **names**: the listener is essentially requested to infer an implicit set description from the names of objects in the set. What I wonder is whether "one" might also be used to access a description inferable off the **descriptions** of objects in a set, basically an ISA (i.e. a superset) inference. All the examples of this that I have so far come up with seem either bad, awkward or incomplete, e.g.

55a. At the Paris zoo, Bruce saw a lion, a tiger, a giraffe, a
     hippopotamus and an elephant.
  b. It was feeding time, and the carnivorous **ones** were eating boeuf
     bourgignon and the herbivorous **ones**, salad nicoise.
     one =? animal

56a. Alongside the trail were an elm, a hickory, two pines, a sugar
     maple and a white oak.
  b. The deciduous **ones** were putting on a good show before the
     arrival of winter.
     one =? tree

Listeners will agree that the examples are understandable, although they don't like them very much. However, it doesn't seem reasonable to believe that examples which require superset inferences could not crop up. It may be a matter of memory strategies, which can vary from situation to situation and person to person. Such strategies would involve ways of inclusively characterizing things **on presentation** in order to remember them. Durkheimer Feuerberg '75, I classify as a wine on presentation. A lion, I classify as just a lion (not "an animal"). But this is pure speculation. <*14>

<*14>. Speculation aided and abetted by Bill Woods.

7. Summary

The main points of this chapter are the following:

a. I have suggested that a "one"-anaphor substitutes for a description presumed to be accessible to both participants in the discourse;

b. I have discussed three different sources for accessible descriptions;

c. I have fit my view of "one"-anaphora into a broad approach to reference which takes as basic the participants' discourse models and their shared conceptualizations of the world;

d. I have suggested two possible representations of English sentences which could be exploited for candidate antecedents for "one"-anaphora. These were a sentence's syntactic parse tree and its Level-2 representation. I have shown how the latter might be processed in order to identify those candidate antecedents.

e. I have demonstrated some types of inferences which operate on explicitly given descriptions to provide additional antecedent descriptions for "one"-anaphora.

TABLE OF CONTENTS

CHAPTER 4. Verb Phrase Ellipsis

1. Introduction

Recall that my major concern in this thesis is in identifying what a text makes available for anaphoric reference and how it does so. My claims are (1) that anaphoric reference cannot be understood in purely linguistic terms - i.e., without appealing to the discourse participants' models of the discourse - and (2) that if a discourse participant does not characterize the formal structure of each new utterance, then s/he will not be able to identify all of what the text makes available for reference. Having discussed definite pronoun and "one" anaphora in the preceding chapters, I shall now turn to a third type of anaphora, namely verb phrase ellipsis and show how these claims are justified here as well. Sentences that illustrate verb phrase ellipsis include

1a. John sings himself to sleep.
 b. Mary does 0 too. <*1>
    0 = sing herself to sleep

2a. John didn't bake a cake for Mary.
 b. Fred did **0**, but she didn't like it.
    0 = bake a cake for Mary.

3a. John hit his mother.
 b. Fred did **0** too.
    0 = hit John's mother
        hit his own mother

4. Wendy wants to sail around the world and Bruce wants to climb Mt. Fuji, but neither of them will **0** if money is too tight.
   0 = do what s/he wants to do

1.1 Historical Context

I shall first review Sag's [1976] account of verb phrase ellipsis <*2> which I mentioned only briefly in Chapter 1, Section 3.3. Sag's essential point is that verb phrase ellipsis is conditioned by identical predicates at a level of "logical form" [Chomsky, 1975a&b]. <*3> In

---

<*1>. **0** stands for the ellipsed verb phrase.
<*2>. Sag calls it "verb phrase deletion" or VPD.
<*3>. According to Chomsky, logical form is both a grammatical stage in the derivation of sentences and a particular representation whose

Sag's version of logical form, a surface verb phrase is represented as a single structural constituent by the use of the abstraction (lambda) operator. This "lambda predicate" is written as applying to the logical form representation of the surface subject noun phrase, e.g.

5. Betsy loves Peter.
   Betsy, $\lambda(s)$[s love Peter]

According to Sag [1976], the structural description of the verb phrase deletion transformation is simply

$$X - AUX - \underset{\downarrow}{VP} - Y$$
$$0$$

where AUX stands for the sentence auxiliary and X and Y are arbitrary string variables. The condition for applying this rule to delete some verb phrase in a sentence is that the "logical form" representation of that verb phrase be identical to that of a syntactically permitted antecedent - i.e., one that does not violate the "backwards anaphora constraint". The rule as stated can match (and subsequently delete) any verb phrase which is preceded by an auxiliary - a main clause verb phrase, a relative clause verb phrase, a subordinate clause verb phrase or even an infinitival or gerundive verb phrase. <#4>

Citing identity of predication allows Sag to account for many hitherto problematic examples, including both the ambiguity of sentence 3b. following the seemingly unambiguous 3a. <#5>

3a. John hit his mother.
  b. Fred did **0** too
     0 = hit John's mother
        hit his own mother

---

structure is critical to certain principles of "universal grammar" that Chomsky wants to assert. According to Chomsky, logical form mediates between surface structure and meaning and is the level at which general principles of intra-sentential anaphora apply [Chomsky, 1975a: p.241]. No comprehensive syntax and semantics have yet been articulated for "logical form".

<#4>. Verb phrase deletion or ellipsis is standardly characterized by this fact that the sentence auxiliary survives the ellipsis. Thus sentence fragments without an auxiliary - e.g. fragments (i) or (ii) - will not be explicated under a treatment of verb phrase ellipsis.
    -- Did Hamlet kill Polonius?
       (i) Gertrude?
       (ii) Why?
<#5>. This has been called the "sloppy identity" problem [Ross 1967].

and the presence of an ellipsed verb phrase within its apparent antecedent as in example 6.

    6. I will read everything that you do **0**.
       0 = read

This latter example was inexplicable given the then standard formulation of the verb phrase deletion transformation, i.e..

$$X - VP - Y - VP - Z$$
$$\Downarrow$$
$$0$$

However, it appears that merely citing identity of logical form is insufficient to account comprehensively for verb phrase ellipsis. It is insufficient from a linguistic viewpoint in that it leaves many instances of verb phrase ellipsis unexplained. (I gave several such examples in Chapter 1, Section 3.3 and will return to this point shortly.) Moreover, it is insufficient from a systems point of view in that it leaves unanswered several critical questions:

1. Can a sentence be deterministically assigned a **single** correct "logical form" which will always account for intuitions that its predicate is the trigger for a subsequent instance of verb phrase ellipsis? <*6>

2. If not, what is to be done?

3. What would constitute an adequate procedure for finding the antecedent of an ellipsed verb phrase?

Although I shall argue in Section 2 that the answer to the first question is no, I shall also make some proposals aimed at what is to be done. In Section 3, I shall describe some constraints on possible antecedents which can be used to simplify the implementation of an effective search procedure, thereby answering in part question 3.

As far as the linguistic incompleteness of Sag's account of verb phrase ellipsis, the problem is that it leaves out those cases where the intuitively correct antecedent seems to

---

<*6>. Following Sag [1976], I will often use the term "trigger" or "ellipsis trigger" for the predicate which conditions verb phrase ellipsis under "identity of predication". Additional terminology includes defining the "source" of a trigger to be the English clause in whose interpretation it appears. I will reserve the term "antecedent" for the English string that is missing from the ellipsed verb phrase. For any given ellipsed verb phrase then, its antecedent will be a contextually appropriate English translation of its ellipsis trigger.

arise from the speaker's deeper understanding of one or more sentences
of the recent discourse. For example,

7. Mary is going to Spain and Fred is going to Australia, but
   neither of them will **0**, if there's a recession.
   0 = go to the place he or she is planning to go to

8. Irv and Mary want to dance together, but Mary can't 0, since her
   husband is here.
   0 = dance with Irv

9. Mary wants to go to Spain and Fred wants to go to Peru, but
   because of limited resources only one of them can **0**.
   0 = go to the place s/he wants to go

In Section 5, I will show that such examples can be treated with respect
to the same formal meaning representation language as before, but doing
so requires abandoning a static view of verb   phrase   ellipsis.
Specifically, I will contend that predicates that are derivable from a
limited class of **inferable** propositions may be used as ellipsis triggers
as well.

1.2 Chapter Organization

     The organization of this chapter reflects what I feel is necessary
in the design of a complete system for resolving verb phrase ellipsis.
In Section 2 I will characterize some properties of ellipsis   triggers.
The presentation will alternate between examples that point out the need
for a particular kind of ellipsis trigger and my proposals for
representing a clause in such a way that its predicate required
trigger.   These proposals, I will claim, are consistent with a simple
syntactic variant of the Level-2 representation introduced in Chapter 2.
There will be several examples here which show that the same English
clause can serve as the source of several different ellipsis triggers.
In these cases, rather than assigning the clause all the necessary
representations explicitly, I will describe procedures for deriving
these other ones from its basic Level-2 representation.

     In Section 3, I will step back from focussing internally on clauses
to consider the question of where to look for the possible triggers of a
particular ellipsed verb phrase. I will present some simple heuristics
which can be used to guide a search procedure, thereby hopefully
reducing the amount of computation required.

In Section 4, I will sketch out a procedure for resolving ellipsed verb phrases which takes into account such a search procedure as well as the derivational procedures discussed in Section 2. I will also discuss here how resolving ellipsed verb phrases fits in with resolving definite pronouns (cf. Chapter 2, Section 6).

In Section 5, I will consider inadequacies in the above presentation brought about by cases where the correct ellipsis trigger is part of some assertion inferable from the explicit discourse, rather than part of the explicit discourse itself.

2. System Requirements: Representational & Procedural

If one accepts that much of verb phrase ellipsis can be accounted for by "identity of predication" within some formal representation of the discourse, then one is obliged both to characterize the appearance of predicates within that formalism (i.e., the syntax and lexicon of the formalism vis a vis predicates) and to specify how they come about. That is my intention in this section. I shall argue that if procedures are to be able to derive all and only the formally possible triggers for a given instance of verb phrase ellipsis, at least the following conventions should be observed: <*7>

1. The surface subject of a clause should be indicated in the representation, as well as its semantic role vis a vis the predicate (Section 2.1).

2. The two different roles that a pronoun can fill - bound variable and discourse entity anaphor - should be kept representationally distinct (Section 2.2).

3. Some indication of an explicit pronoun should be left in the representation if the pronoun was resolved against a discourse entity, rather than standing for a bound variable (Section 2.2).

4. Existentially quantified subjects should be represented in terms of the discourse entities they evoke, rather than as quantifiers (Section 2.3).

5. Other existentially quantified noun phrases should be accessible both as quantifiers and in terms of the discourse entities they evoke (Section 2.3).

<*7>. At least one area which I have not considered comprises the various types of adverbials. Thus I cannot state their representational or processing requirements vis a vis verb phrase ellipsis.

6. A clause with an explicit negative in its auxiliary should be represented as a general negated proposition (at least for these procedures), even if the reason for the negative is known or suspected (Section 2.4).

7. The cardinality of a plural subject should not be included as part of the predicate (Section 2.5).

8. One should be able to treat individuals as singleton sets (Section 2.5).

9. When "each" follows a subject noun phrase, it should be represented as a universal quantifier within the predicate, not as part of the subject (Section 2.5).

10. A non-subject relative clause should be considered a predicate on both its syntactic subject and relative head which fills some other syntactic role (e.g., direct object, prepositional object, etc.). Resolving ellipsed non-subject relatives therefore requires a syntactic procedure for re-writing clauses with unary predicates into ones with binary predicates as constituents (Section 2.6).

What I shall show is that a simple syntactic variant of the Level-2 representation introduced in Chapter 2 allows one to make these distinctions.

2.1 Surface Subjects

The simplest point to make about an adequate representation of a simple active or passive clause <*8> is that its surface subject be identifiable. (The same point has been made by Sag [1976].) There are two reasons for this: the first is simply be able to exclude the subject from any predicate that might be derived from the clause. The second is that existentials in subject position must be treated specially, as I shall discuss in Section 2.2.

Another point about surface subject is that its logical role vis a vis the predicate must be identified. <*9> For convenience, I shall

---

<*8>. I am ignoring here all stress-related structures like
        Betsy, Peter likes.
        It is Betsy who Peter likes.
        Who Peter likes is Betsy.
since I do not think they yield ellipsis triggers in the same way as simple actives or passives. I shall confine my remarks about verb phrase ellipsis to simple actives and passives, to-complements, etc.
<*9>. I am drawing here on linguistic notions of the **logical argument structure** of a verb, cf. [Bresnan, 1978].

assume that the logical subject of a predicate will always be its first argument, that its logical object will be its second arguments, etc. The specific reason for identifying the logical role of a clause's surface subject is to reduce the search space of possible triggers for a given ellipsed verb phrase. That is, the subject of the ellipsed verb phrase must fill the same logical role with respect to the ellipsis trigger as the trigger's own subject does. This comes out most clearly in the case of multiple passive forms. For example, "give" has two different passives: in one, the syntactic subject is the logical indirect object, in the other, it is the logical object, cf.

10a. Wendy was given a banana by a woman I know.
   b. A banana was given to Wendy by a woman I know.

If the representations of these two sentences only differed in which noun phrase filled the surface subject - i.e., the logical role of that noun phrase was not also identified, then it would not be clear why examples 11a&b. sound strange while examples 11c&d do not.

11a. Wendy was given a banana for her birthday, and an apple was O too.
   b. A banana was given to Wendy for her birthday, and Phyllis was O too.
   c. Wendy was given a banana for her birthday, and Phyllis was O too.
   d. A banana was given to Wendy for her birthday, and an apple was O too.

I am going to jump in here and claim that in a simple syntactic variant of the Level-2 representation of a sentence, the surface subject of that sentence can be distinguished. Moreover, all the other distinctions to be discussed in the following sections can be made as well. In this variant, clauses are indicated for the most part (the one exception to be discussed in Section 2.6) in terms of complex unary predicates applied to the interpretation of the surface subject. <*10> So whereas I had been writing the Level-2 interpretation of a sentence like "A woman I know dislikes Peter" as

(Ex:λ(u:W)[Know I,u]) . Dislike x, Peter

<*10>. This will resemble somewhat Sag's "logical form" representation described earlier.

(where W stands for woman), I will now write it as

    (Ex:λ(u:W)[I, λ(r)[Know r,u]]) . x, λ(s)[Dislike s, Peter]

Actives and passives, which differ in which logical role fills the surface subject, will differ in which argument appears as the argument to the lambda predicate. For example,

    12. Bruce bought a mini-computer
        Bruce, λ(r)[(Ex:Mini) . Bought r,x]

    13. A min-computer was bought by Bruce.
        (Ex:Mini) . x, λ(r)[Bought Bruce,r]

(This variant of the Level-2 representation in terms of lambda predicates - as well as a similar variant of the Level-1 representation - are both longer to write and harder to read than the "flatter" forms given earlier. They also make the precise specification of the ID-rule slightly more complicated. Thus I have avoided using them up to now. Notice that the flatter representation can be derived from this "lambda predicate" form by a simple mechanical process.)

2.2 Pronouns

In this section I shall discuss how definite pronouns must be represented and processed in order to guarantee an adequate treatment of verb phrase ellipsis. (This will be completely compatible with my remarks in Chapter 2, Section 6 on definite pronoun resolution, since they were made with VP ellipsis in mind as well.)

I shall argue that the two different roles that a definite pronoun can fill must be distinguishable representationally <*11> although one may want to keep them merged most of the time since they most often coincide. It is only when the effects of the two roles diverge - such as in the case of "sloppy identity", to be discussed next - that one must acknowledge that a pronoun can play one or the other role separately as well as together. I shall show that this temporary merging is facilitated by leaving some trace of an explicit pronoun in the Level-2 representation following the pronoun's resolution against a

---

<*11>. Recall from Chapter 1, Section 5 that definite pronouns can be used to refer to discourse entities **or** they can function as bound variables, implying that two or more argument places within an expression are to be filled identically.

discourse entity. That is, I shall argue that a pronoun should not be blindly replaced by some indication of its referent without leaving a trace. <*12>

The problem of "sloppy identity" [Ross, 1967] is to account for the ambiguity of a sentence with an ellipsed verb phrase, when the source of its antecedent seems unambiguous. Cases of "sloppy identity" appear when that source sentence has one or more definite pronouns in its verb phrase that are co-referential with its subject. The following is a simple example of "sloppy identity".

    14a. Garth beats his wife.
      b. Fred does 0 too.

sentence 14a. seems unambiguous, sentence 14b. might mean either that Fred beats Garth's wife or that he beats his own.

To show how this ambiguity comes about, I will begin by supposing that sentence 14a. can be assigned the Level-1 representation

        Garth, $\lambda(r)$[Beat r, wife-of(HE)]

(where "wife-of" is a function from individuals to individuals). <*13> I will also suppose that the sentence intends to convey that Garth's wife is the victim (i.e., "he"=Garth). Notice however, that this supposition can be made on one of two bases: either HE refers to that discourse entity describable as "the person named Garth" or HE stands for the bound variable r and indicates that whatever fills the subject of "Beat" also fills the argument to "wife-of".

<*12>. This view of how pronouns should be represented resembles that presented in [Sag 1976]. Where it differs is in how that representation is processed.

<*13>. An alternative representation for possessives was suggested in [Nash-Webber & Reiter, 1977]. In that paper, we introduced **'s** as a function from unary predicates to unary functions. For example, **'s**(Wife) is a function that takes as its argument an expression that refers to a man and returns an expression that refers to his wife: **'s**(Wife)Garth refers to Garth's wife. Having **'s** available eliminates the need to postulate a separate "Y-of" function for every unary predicate "Y". Moreover Y need not be a predicate that has already been named (e.g. Wife, Boy, etc.): it can be one that has been constructed using the abstraction operator. For example, **'s**(λ(r:T-shirt)[Green r])Garth refers to Garth's green T-shirt. I will not be using **'s** here because I haven't yet had the opportunity to explore all of its implications.

Under the discourse referent assumption, the Level-2 interpretation of sentence 14a. can be written

   Garth, $\lambda(r)$[Beat r, wife-of(PRO=Garth)]

using the syntactic construction PRO=<de>, where <de> is either the label of a discourse entity (e.g. e_{74}) or a definite description (e.g. "Garth"). PRO stands for "pronoun" unmarked for either gender or number. (I shall argue later why such markings are unproductive once the pronoun has been resolved.) Under the semantics of an expression containing an instance of PRO=<de> is exactly that of one containing <de> alone. The reason for introducing PRO=<de> rather than simply **replacing** a pronoun with <de> will be given very shortly.

Under the bound variable assumption, the Level-2 representation of sentence 14a. can be written

   Garth, $\lambda(r)$[Beat r, wife-of(r)]

In this case, the pronoun has been replaced completely, reflecting its role as a simple place-holder.

The point about these alternative representations of sentence 14a., which are semantically equivalent in the given case, is that they supply two quite different antecedents subsequent ellipsed verb phrase: on the one hand,

   $\lambda(r)$[Beat r, wife-of(PRO=Garth)]

i.e., "beating Garth's wife" and on the other,

   $\lambda(r)$[Beat r, wife-of(r)]

i.e., "beating one's own wife". This accounts for the "sloppy identity" problem since these are the two possible antecedents of the ellipsed verb phrase in sentence 14b., "Fred does 0 too".

Given though that a sentence like 14a. is unambiguous on its own, it is useful to be able to keep its alternative forms merged until it is accessed as a source of possible ellipsis triggers (cf. Section 3). Since, as I shall argue below, it is necessary to record the original presence of a pronoun referring to a discourse entity, and since the bound variable form can be derived from the "PRO=" form by a simple rewrite rule like

[RW-1]   s, λ(r)[P...PRO=s...] => s,   (r)[P...r...]

where PRO=s may occur any number of times, at any depth of embedding, it is reasonable to include the "PRO=" form as part of the standard Level-2 representation. <*14>

I shall next present three reasons why some trace of a resolved pronoun (e.g. PRO=e_k) appear in the Level-2 representation. The first reason will explain why representing pronoun-referent pairs explicitly is preferable to merely **replacing** the pronoun with the label of its referent. The second reason will explain why it is preferable predicate/bound variable representation. The third reason will explain why an unmarked PRO is preferable to the original pronoun marked for gender and number.

(1) If a pronoun were merely replaced by a pointer to its discourse entity referent, the resulting expression would be indistinguishable from the representation of a sentence containing a definite description reference to that entity. However sentences with definite descriptions behave differently with respect to verb phrase ellipsis from ones containing definite pronouns. For example,

16a. Only John wanted Mary to kiss John.
  b. Fred didn't **0**.
     0 = want Mary to kiss John
     $\neq$ want Mary to kiss Fred

17a. Only John wanted Mary to kiss him.
  b. Fred didn't **0**.
     0 = want Mary to kiss him (John)
        = want Mary to kiss him (Fred)

<*14>. There is a discussion in [Sag 1976, Chapter 2.2] that suggests a constraint on [RW-1] based on Chomsky's [1975b] constraint barring logical structures in which a bound variable is preceded by a pro-form related to it anaphorically. That is, if a sentence is understood to contain several instances of PRO=s, e.g.
  (i) Wendy gave her sister a book she liked.
      Wendy, λ(r)[(Ex:λ(u:Book)[Like PRO=Wendy,u])
           Gave r, sister-of(PRO=Wendy)]
then if [RW-1] replaces the jth instance of PRO=s by the bound variable, then all previous j-1 instances of PRO=s must be replaced as well. That is, the ellipsed verb phrase in "Phyllis did **0** too" following (i) cannot have among its possible antecedents "gave her (own) sister a book she=Wendy liked".

18a. The king may hunt on the king's land.
  b. The prince may 0 too.
     0 = hunt on the king's land.
     0 ≠ hunt on his own land.

Sentences 16a. and 18a. each has its subject noun phrase repeated in its
verb phrase. As can be seen by the b. sentences following them, neither
allows a sloppy reading of the ellipsed verb phrase. Sentence 17a.,
containing a definite pronoun instead, does admit the possibility of a
sloppy reading of its following ellipsed VP sentence. Therefore,
definite pronouns must be distinguished from definite noun phrases.

(2) If the lambda predicate/bound variable form were chosen as the
Level-2 representation of a sentence, the resulting expression would be
indistinguishable from that of an "equi" sentence. <*15> Such
sentences also behave differently with respect to verb phrase ellipsis
than do pronoun-containing ones. For example,

19a. John wanted to win.
  b. Fred didn't **0**.
     0 = want himself to win
       ≠ want John to win

20a. John wanted his father to win.
  b. Fred didn't **0**.
     0 = want his (own) father to win
       = want John's father to win

Sentence 19a. illustrates an "equi" sentence. The ellipsed verb phrase
sentence which follows it is unambiguous, admitting only a bound
variable sense. The ellipsed verb phrase sentence following the
pronoun-containing sentence (example 20) admits two readings. Adopting
a lambda predicate/bound variable base representation for all sentences
containing definite pronouns would mean either that "equi" sentences
would be assigned a reading inappropriate to them or that "sloppy"
readings could not be derived for the others (or, of course, that "equi"
sentences would have to marked in some other way).

(3) While it isn't necessary to have a single genderless,
numberless way of indicating pronoun-referent pairs, having one means

---

<*15>. An "equi" sentence is one which contains a "to"-complement whose
implicit subject or object is necessarily co-referential ("equi") with
the subject noun phrase of the matrix.

that a single rewrite rule like [RW-1] can be defined for going   from   a
"PRO=" form   to   a   bound variable form.   Notice that the bound variable
form makes no reference to either   the   gender   or   the   number   of   the
original   pronoun.   This is consistent with the fact that these original
markings seem to be irrelevant for sloppy readings, e.g.

    21a. John loves **his** mother.
      b. Mary does **0** too.
        0 = loves **her** mother (or loves John's mother)

    22a. John loves **his** mother.
      b. His twin cousins do **0** too.
        0 = love **their** mother (or love John's mother)

However whether one wants several conversion rules (one for each kind of
marked pronoun), one conversion   rule   parameterized   for   all   pronouns
(regardless   of   markings), or one conversion rule and a single unmarked
pronoun may really only be a matter of convenience.   At any rate for the
"sloppy identity" phenomenon, pronoun markings for gender and number are
not necessary after the pronouns have been resolved.

2.3 Existential Quantifiers

    In this section, I   shall   argue   for   a   particular   treatment   of
existentially   quantified sentences in order to account for instances of
verb phrase ellipsis such as those that follow. <*16>   (This   treatment
will   of   course   be   compatible   with   the   discussion   of   existential
quantifiers in Chapter 2.)

    23. A famous Boston author wanted me to like him. My brother did **0**
        too.
        0 = want me to like that author
           want me to like my brother
           want me to like some entity referenced previously

    24. A famous Boston author wanted me to like him because Wendy
        didn't **0**.
        0 = like that author
           like some entity referenced previously

The problem illustrated in these examples is that if "he" is treated
simply as the variable bound by the existential quantifier corresponding
to "a famous Boston author" - i.e.,

<*16>. Similar examples containing a universal quantifier I usually
find   strange.   As   the   data   are   not   as   straightforward   as in the
existential case, I shall put off considering them.

(Ex:**A**) . x, $\lambda(r)$[Want r, {I, $\lambda(s)$[Like s,r]}]

(where **A** stands for "famous Boston author"), then the only potential ellipsis trigger is

(i) $\lambda(r)$[Want r, {I, $\lambda(s)$[Like s,r]}]

i.e., "wanting me to like whoever it is doing the wanting". On the other hand, if "he" refers to some previously evoked discourse entity e_k, then the only potential ellipsis triggers are

(ii) $\lambda(r)$[Want r, {I, $\lambda(s)$[Like s, PRO=e_k]}]
     "wanting me to like that person"

(iii) $\lambda(s)$[Like s, PRO=e_k]
      "liking that person"

Neither of these accounts for the possibilities "wanting me to like that author" or "liking that author".

However these possibilities can be accounted for under the following proposal, as can the possibility labelled (i). I propose that for a non-negative sentence with an existentially quantified subject, the form of Level-2 representation accessed for ellipsis triggers be the referential form (cf. Chapter 2, Sections 3&6) in which the quantifier is replaced by the label of the discourse entity it evokes. <*17> (After this I shall argue that both types of Level-2 representation - referential and quantifier - are required for other existentials.)

According to this proposal, in examples 23 and 24 the form of Level-2 representation accessed for ellipsis triggers would be

(A) e_1, $\lambda(r)$[Want r, {I, $\lambda(s)$[Like s, PRO=e_1]}]

where e_1 is the entity evoked by the subject position existential describable as

---

<*17>. The reason for the non-negative restriction is that existentials within the scope of negation do not evoke discourse entities (cf. Chapter 2, Section 5.4). Thus no specific one would appear in an ellipsis trigger. The account I give here is partially confirmed by the fact that there is no corresponding reading for the ellipsed verb phrase in this case either, e.g.

   - No famous Boston author wanted me to like him. But my father
     did **0**.
   0 = *wanted me to like him=that author,
         wanted me to like him=my father

ix: **Ax** & x,λ(r)[Want r, {I, λ(s)[Like s,r]}] & **evoke** S_{24},x

i.e., "the just-mentioned famous Boston author who wants me to like him". (This is assuming that "he" does not refer to some previously evoked discourse entity e_k. In that case, the Level-2 representation accessed for ellipsis triggers would be

(B) e_1, λ(r)[Want r, {I, λ(s)[Like s, PRO=e_k]}]   ).

Notice that the form of (A) is exactly that of the "sloppy identity" cases discussed earlier. As such, there are several predicates identifiable as potential ellipsis triggers

(iv) λ(r)[Want r, {I, λ(s)[Like s, PRO=e_1]}]
    "wanting me to like e_1 (i.e. that author)

(v) λ(s)[Like s, PRO=e_1]
    "liking e_1"
as well as

(i) λ(r)[Want r, {I, λ(s)[Like s,r]}

(The predicates labelled (ii) and (iii) are derivable from (B) in that case where the referent of "he" is some previously evoked discourse entity.) Thus the referential Level-2 representation of examples 23-24 allows one to account for all the possibly intended antecedents of their ellipsed verb phrases.

As for needing both forms of Level-2 representation - quantifier and referential - for predicate-based existentials, the reason is that either representation alone will not provide all the potential ellipsis triggers. For example, consider the sentence

25. At the party I met a famous Boston author and Wendy did **0** too.
    0 = met that person, met a famous Boston author

The referential Level-2 representation of the first clause can be written

I, λ(r)[Met r, e_2, "at the party"]

(finessing the representation of the adverbial), where e_2 is the discourse entity describable as "the just-mentioned famous Boston author I met at the party". In this case, the only potential ellipsis trigger would be

λ(r)[Met r, e_2, "at the party"]

i.e., "meeting that author at the party". On the other hand, the
quantifier Level-2 representation of the first clause can be written

   I, $\lambda(r)[(Ex:A)$. Met r,x,"at the party"]

In this case, the only possible ellipsis trigger would be

   $\lambda(r)[(Ex:A)$. Met r,x,"at the party"]

i.e., "meeting a famous Boston author at the party".

Now while both forms of Level-2 representation are needed as
sources of ellipsis triggers, I would suggest keeping only one around
explicitly until the sentence was suggested as a potential source. The
representation I would suggest is the version in which predicate
existentials are represented as quantifiers since, with every clause
tagged with the discourse entities it evokes (cf. Chapter 2, Section 6),
the possibly several discourse entity versions can be easily derived.

Notice that this dual treatment of predicate existentials also
permits a clean account of Sag's observation [1976] (following Kuno
[1974]) that verb phrase ellipsis is insensitive to existential
specificity. That is, both Sag and Kuno have observed that it is
possible to interpret a noun phrase in an ellipsed verb phrase
non-specifically while the corresponding noun phrase in its antecedent
is interpreted specifically. Sag gives as an example

   26. Jane ended up marrying a doctor, although she didn't want to.

His claim is that the noun phrase "a doctor" in the explicit verb phrase
can only be interpreted specifically, i.e. as the specific doctor who
Jane ended up marrying. However, the clause containing the ellipsed
verb phrase may be interpreted in either of two different ways:

   ...although she didn't want to **marry a doctor** (non-specific)
   or
   ...although she didn't want to **marry that doctor** (specific)

Sag takes the first as evidence of the insensitivity of verb phrase
ellipsis to existential specificity (i.e., specific existential in the
trigger, non-specific in the target). Although I feel that specificity
itself is more a matter of pragmatic concern (cf. Chapter 2,
Section 2.1), the simple point I shall demonstrate here is how these two
different antecedents - "marry a doctor" and "marry that doctor" fall
out of this elsewhere needed dual treatment of predicate existentials.

Rather than looking at Sag's example, I will consider the sentence pair

27a. Jane married a doctor.
   b. However, she didn't want to **0**.

in which the first sentence is similarly unambiguous, and the second, similarly ambiguous. In this way, I can ignore material irrelevant to the point, as well as any possible account involving wide vs. narrow quantifier scope for "a doctor".

In processing this pair, sentence 27a. would first be assigned the Level-2 representation

$$\text{Jane, } \lambda(r)[(\text{Ex:Doctor}) \text{ . Married } r,x]$$

It would then be processed for discourse entities via the ID-rule given in Chapter 2 and tagged with the two of them that it evokes - e_1, describable as "the person named Jane" and e_2, describable as

$$\text{ix:Doctor x \& Married Jane,x \& } \textbf{evoke } S_{27a.},x$$

i.e., "the just-mentioned doctor Jane married".

Moving on, sentence 27b. would be assigned a Level-1 representation like

however ~ SHE, $\lambda(s)[\text{Want } s, \{P? \ s\}]$

(Recall from the previous section that "want to X" exemplifies an "equi" construction: the subject of its "to"-complement is always co-referential with its subject - hence the bound variable representation.) If sentence 27a. were then searched for possible triggers for the ellipsed verb phrase, two predicates would be found. Resolving P? against the one derived from the quantifier representation of 27a. would result in

however ~ SHE, $\lambda(s)[\text{Want } s, \{s, \lambda(r)[(\text{Ex:D}) \text{ . M } r,x]\}]$

i.e., "However, she didn't want to marry a doctor". Resolving P? against the predicate derivable from the referential Level-2 representation of 27a would result in

however ~ SHE, $\lambda(s)[\text{Want } s, \{s, \lambda(r)[\textbf{M } r,e_2]\}]$

i.e., "However, she didn't want to marry that doctor". The problem now for the understanding system is that of deciding the speaker-intended sense. Whether the system's inability to make an immediate decision on this point creates a problem will depend on how existentials in modal contexts are processed. (Unfortunately I have not had the opportunity to give this problem much thought, cf. Chapter 2, Section 5.4.)

2.4 Negation

Even if it is possible to assign a more precise reading (and consequently a more precise representation) to a sentence with an explicit negative in its auxiliary, the Level-2 form of that sentence accessed as a source of possible ellipsis triggers should be that containing full propositional negation. For example, even if the listener knows that

28. John didn't marry a Swedish girl.
    ~ John, $\lambda(r)[(Ex: \lambda(u:Girl)[Swedish\ u])$. Marry r,x]

is true because the person John married wasn't Swedish or that the person wasn't a girl or that he didn't marry anyone, etc. (cf. Chapter 2, Section 5.4), it remains the case that the only unary predicate derivable from sentence 28 that can serve as the antecedent for an ellipsed verb phrase is

$\lambda(r)[(Ex: \lambda(u:Girl)[Swedish\ u])$. Marry r,x]

i.e. "marrying a Swedish girl". If sentence 28 were followed by either "but Fred did 0" or "and neither did Fred 0", it would only be to imply that Fred married a Swedish girl or that Fred didn't marry a Swedish girl either without commitment to any more specific interpretation of the negative.

2.5 Plurals

In this section I want to consider some aspects of the representation and processing of plural noun phrases necessary for an adequate treatment of verb phrase ellipsis. Sentences illustrating the points I plan to make include:

29. Because three men ate four pizzas, Bruce did 0 too.
    0 = ate four pizzas

30. Because the boys hit their sisters, Wendy did 0 too.
    0 = hit those boys' sisters
      = hit her own sister(s)
      = hit the sisters of the same previously mentioned entities
        as did the boys

31. Because the boys hit their sisters, the girls did 0 too.
    0 = hit those boys' sisters
      = (collectively) hit their own sisters
      = hit the sisters of the same previously mentioned entities
        as did the boys
      = each hit her own sister(s)

32. Because the three men each ate four pizzas, the five girls did 0
    too.
    0 = each ate four pizzas

33. Because the three men each ate four pizzas, Sally did 0 too.
    0 = ate four pizzas

The first point illustrated in example 29 (repeated below) is that no matter how cardinality is indicated, the cardinality of the subject noun phrase should never be mistaken for part of the predicate.

29. Because three men ate four pizzas, Bruce did 0 too.

If the Level-2 representation of the first clause is

$(Ex:\textbf{set}(\textbf{M}))$. x, $\lambda(r)[(Ey:\textbf{set}(\textbf{P}))$. Eat r,y & $|y|=4]$ & $|x|=3$

(where $\textbf{M}$ stands for "man" and $\textbf{P}$, for "pizza"), then only the predicate corresponding to the actual verb phrase should be picked up as a possible ellipsis trigger - i.e.,

$\lambda(r)[(Ey:\textbf{set}(\textbf{P}))$. Eat r,y & $|y|=4]$
    "eat four pizzas"

The term $|x|=3$ must not appear as part of that predicate.

Another way to avoid picking up subject cardinality is to adopt the proposal I made earlier to access the referential Level-2 representation of a sentence when its subject was existentially quantified, cf.

e_1, $\lambda(r)[(Ey:\textbf{set}(\textbf{P}))$. Eat r,y & $|y|=4]$

where e_1 is the discourse entity describable as

ix:$\textbf{set}(\textbf{M})$x & $|x|=3$ & $(Ey:\textbf{set}(\textbf{P}))$. Eat x,y & $|y|=4$
        & evoke $S_{29.1}$,x

i.e., "the just-mentioned set of three men that ate four pizzas". In this way, subject cardinality is not part of the representation accessed for ellipsis triggers and ignoring it raises no problem.

The other point illustrated by example 29 is that verb phrase ellipsis is insensitive to whether a predicate applies to individuals or to sets. That is, in the first clause of example 29, the predicate

$\lambda(r)[(Ey:\textbf{set}(P))$. Ate r,y & $|y|=4]$

gets a set as its argument. However, it can act as the trigger for verb phrase ellipsis in "Bruce did **0** too", where it takes an individual as its argument. Thus a search for ellipsis triggers cannot be limited to only predicates on individuals or only predicates on sets.

Some predicates of course only make sense when applied to either individuals or to sets. This is the case by virtue of their lexical rather than their formal semantics (e.g. "gather", "pile up", etc.). But in order not to ignore potential ellipsis triggers, it is probably best to use such a constraint as a filter later on.

There is another way to look at this insensitivity - i.e., in terms of individuals as singleton sets. Consider example 30.

30. Because the boys hit their sisters, Wendy did **0** too.
    0 = hit those boys' sisters
        = hit her own sister(s)
        = hit the sisters of the same previously mentioned entities
          as did the boys

This is essentially another case of "sloppy identity" (cf. Section 2.2). Where it differs from earlier examples is that while the first clause makes no claims about whose (or how many) sisters any one boy hit, just as long as each person hit was the sister of one of those boys (or one of some previously mentioned entities), the second clause seems to claim that Wendy hit either all her own sister(s) or all of the sisters of the previously mentioned entities.

Consider how this sentence would be processed. Initially its first clause would be assigned the Level-1 representation

ix:**maxset**(**B**)x, $\lambda(r)[$Hit r,iy:**maxset**$(\lambda(s)[(Ez \in THEY)$. sister-of(z)s])y]

where **B** stands for boy and "sister-of" is a function from individuals to predicates. If the definite description "the boys" is found to be anaphoric, this can be written as

(i) e_1, $\lambda(r)[$Hit r, iy:**maxset**$(\lambda(s)[(Ez \in THEY)$. sister-of(z)s])y]

Assuming then that "they" refers to e_i (or equivalently here, stands for a bound variable), (i) can be re-written in either of two semantically equivalent ways.

(ii) e_1, $\lambda(r)$[Hit r, iy:**maxset**($\lambda(s)$[(Ez∊PRO=e_1) . sister-of(z)s])y]

(iii) e_1, $\lambda(r)$[Hit r, iy:**maxset**($\lambda(s)$[(Ez∊r) . sister-of(z)s])y]

(As discussed in Section 2.2, the bound variable version (iii) can be derived from the "PRO=" version (ii) by simply applying [RW-1]. Thus it may be left implicit.)

If (ii) is accessed as a source of possible ellipsis triggers for "Wendy did 0 too", the explicit predicate

$\lambda(r)$[Hit r, iy:**maxset**($\lambda(s)$[(Ez∊PRO=e_1) . sister-of(z)s])y]
"hitting those boys' sisters"

will immediately be found. However, if (iii) is then accessed as a source of possible triggers, there will be a problem since the argument to the derived predicate

$\lambda(r)$[Hit r, iy:**maxset**($\lambda(s)$[(Ez∊r) . sister-of(z)s])y]

must clearly be a set in order for the quantifier (Ez r) to make sense. One way out of this is to view the discourse entity (say e_2) describable as "Wendy" as a singleton set, **provided that** it does not affect e_2's status vis a vis definite pronoun anaphora (i.e., it should not be considered as a possible referent for "they"). Viewing e_2 as a singleton set not only makes it appropriate to apply the predicate to it, but also makes the semantics come out right to mean "Wendy hit her own sister(s)".

Now consider example 31 (repeated below)

31. Because the boys hit their sisters, the girls did 0 too.
    0 = hit those boys' sisters
      = (collectively) hit their own sisters
      = hit the sisters of the same previously mentioned entities
        as did the boys
      = each hit her own sister(s)

It is the fourth reading of the ellipsed verb phrase that I am interested in. It seems to me that this reading only appears if the first clause is interpreted narrowly as "Because the boys (each) hit his own sister(s)...". If this narrow interpretation of the first clause is represented as

ix:**maxset**(B)x, $\lambda(r)$[(∀s∊r) . Hit s, iy:**maxset**($\lambda(u)$[sister-of(s)u])y]

then the predicate available as an ellipsis trigger will be the fourth reading above

$\lambda(r)[(\forall s \epsilon r)$. Hit s, iy:**maxset**$(\lambda(u)[sister-of(s)u])y]$

i.e., "each hitting his or her own sister(s)".

Notice here that I have represented the implicit distributive as part of the predicate rather than applying it to the subject, as in

$(\forall y \epsilon ix:Bx)$. y, $\lambda(r)[Hit\ r$, iy:**maxset**$(\lambda(u)[sister-of(r)u])y]$

I have two reasons for doing this. This first is that it simplifies an account of why the ellipsed clause "The girls did 0 too" should be understood distributively as well. (The other way would require that the procedure for resolving verb phrase ellipsis be able to update the interpretation of the subject as well, and I have not seen any other call for such a capability.)

My second reason is that this ability to include the distributive as part of a predicate is also needed to account for instances where an ellipsis trigger comes from a clause in which "each" follows the subject. To see this consider example 32 (repeated below).

32. Because the three men each ate four pizzas, the five women did 0 too.
    0 = each ate four pizzas

The simplest way to account for this intuitively correct antecedent is to view the first clause as predicating of that set of three men "each (member) eating four pizzas" - i.e.,

ix:**maxset**$(M)x$ & $|x|=3$, $\lambda(r)[(\forall s \epsilon r)(Ey:set(P))$. Ate s,y & $|y|=4]$

Then the appropriate ellipsis trigger for the second clause is immediately available.

Finally, to account for cases like example 33 (repeated below)

33. Because the three men each ate four pizzas, Sally did 0 too.
    0 = ate four pizzas

where a clause in which "each" follows the subject provides the ellipsis trigger for a clause with an individual subject, the individual subject can again be viewed as a singleton set (as suggested above) to remove the incompatibility.

2.6 Non-subject Relative Clauses

I mentioned in Section 1.1 Sag's observation that "identity of predication" facilitates a simple explanation of the hitherto problematic case where an ellipsed verb phrase seems to be part of its apparent antecedent. Such a situation can occur when the ellipsis site is a non-subject relative clause, <*18> e.g.,

34. Betsy wants Peter to read everything that Alan does **0**.
    0 = want Peter to read, read [Sag, 1976]

Under Sag's deletion account (and using his notation), a sentence like 34 can reflect either of the following two underlying forms

(i) Betsy, $\lambda(x)[x$ want $\{(\forall y$: Alan, $\lambda(w)[w$ read y])
        Peter, $\lambda(z)[z$ read y]}]

(ii) Betsy, $\lambda(x)[x$ want
        $\{(\forall y$: Alan, $\lambda(z)[z$ want {Peter, $\lambda(w)[w$ read y]}])
        Peter, $\lambda(q)[q$ read y]}]

In each case, the deletion of the surface verb phrase is sanctioned by the pair of identical predicates. In this section, I will be concerned with what is needed in order to recover the identical but unknown predicates which could have triggered the ellipsis.

Consider first sentence 35.

35. Bruce read every book that Wendy did **0**.

The relative clause "that Wendy did **0**" can be viewed as stating a relationship between its subject - "Wendy" - and its relative head - in this case, "book". <*19> Therefore rather than representing non-subject relative clauses (either ellipsed or full) unary predicates, as I have other types of clauses, it seems conceptually more appropriate to represent them in terms of **binary** predicates on the clausal subject and the relative head. (In the following, angle brackets will be used to group these two arguments to the lambda predicate - subject first, relative head second - i.e.,

Bruce, $\lambda(r)[(\forall x:\lambda(u:B)[<Wendy, u>, \lambda(r,s)[P?\ r,s]])\ .\ R\ r,x]$

<*18>. Sag does not identify any other ways in which this situation can arise, nor have I been able to find others myself.

<*19>. In a subject relative clause, the subject and head of the clause coincide. Thus the clause can be viewed as stating a unary property rather than a binary relation.

where **B** stands for "book" and **R** for "read".) The problem is now to resolve the unknown predicate P? by finding an appropriate **binary** predicate which could have sanctioned the elision.

Notice that except for explicit binary predicates like R ("read"), most of the predicates in the Level-2 representation are unary. This is because all clauses except for non-subject relatives are represented in terms of a unary predicate applied to the interpretation of the surface subject (Section 3.1). However, this is a purely syntactic convention, and any clause that can be written in the form

a, λ(r)[P r ...b...]

can also be written as

<a,b>, λ(r,s)[P r...s...]

provided that neither opacity nor scope dependencies are violated. Such a rewrite procedure is what I see as needed for identifying possible antecedents in the case of ellipsis in non-subject relative clauses. <*20>

To illustrate the use of such a rewrite procedure, reconsider example 34.

34. Betsy wants Peter to read every book that Alan does 0.

For me, this sentence has three possible readings, paraphrasable as

a. What Betsy wants is for Peter to read every book that Alan reads.
b. Every book that Alan reads Betsy wants Peter to read. <*21>
c. Every book that Wendy wants Peter to read Betsy wants Peter to read. <*22>

<*20>. This would not be used to actually **change** the representation of a clause, but rather to produce an additional representation in some temporary workspace, if the clause were accessed for possible ellipsis triggers, cf. Section 4.

<*21>. The difference between a. and b. is that Betsy could want the a. reading (but not the b. reading), without knowing each of the books that Alan has read, is reading or will read.

<*22>. Woods [personal communication] has suggested that sentence 34 may also have the reading "What Betsy wants is for Peter to read every book that Alan wants him to read". If so, it is a reading that would not fall out of this treatment. Needless to say, it is not a reading I get.

To begin with, sentence 35 is ambiguous with respect to the scopes of the quantifier "every" and the opaque verb "want". That is, sentence 35 could be represented as either

   (i) Betsy, $\lambda(r)$[W r, {Peter, $\lambda(s)$[($\forall x:\lambda(b:B)$[<Alan, b>, $\lambda(t,u)$[P? t,u]]) . R s,x}]

   (ii) ($\forall x:\lambda(b:B)$[<Alan, b>, $\lambda(t,u)$[P? t,u]])
        Betsy, $\lambda(r)$[W r, {Peter, $\lambda(s)$[R s,x]}]

where W stands for "want", R for "read" and B for "book". (Recall from the previous example that the relative clause "that Wendy does" expresses a (currently unknown) relation between "Wendy", as subject, and "book", as relative head.)

Both (i) and (ii) contain the explicit binary predicate R ("read"). Resolving P? against R yields the a. reading above in the case of (i) and the b. reading above in the case of (ii). Notice however that (ii), but not (i), can also be re-written in terms of the following derived binary predicate, which is another possible ellipsis trigger for P?,

   ($\forall x:\lambda(b:B)$[<Alan b>, $\lambda(t,u)$[P? t,u]])
        <Betsy, x>, $\lambda(p,q)$[W p, {Peter, $\lambda(s)$[R s,q]}]

namely "wanting Peter to reading something". Resolving P? in this way yields the third reading (c.) given above. (Any attempt to rewrite (i) in terms of a binary predicate on "Bruce" and some other argument will either violate the opacity of "want" or leave P? as part of the derived predicate. The latter leads to an untenable recursion.)

3. Surface Constraints on Verb Phrase Ellipsis

This section will discuss four surface constraints which can be used to mitigate the search for possible triggers for a given ellipsed verb phrase: proximity to the ellipsis target, structural position relative to the ellipsis target, the voice (active/passive) of the ellipsis target, and whether or not it is explicitly negated. <*23>

<*23>. I want to emphasize that my remarks concern verb phrase ellipsis as a written phenomenon. In spoken discourse, the strongest cue to the intended antecedent may be stress. However, about stress I cannot speak with any authority. My intuitive reaction is that verb phrase ellipsis is much more intimately linked to language as speech than are the other two types of anaphora discussed earlier. I believe research is currently underway at the University of Massachusetts (Amherst)

These constraints will be more simply statable with respect to a syntactic representation of the discourse sentences than with respect to either a Level-1 or Level-2 semantic representation. This is further evidence for the value of having both syntactic and semantic representations around. I shall also show that there is no simple way at least to use tense and aspect - i.e., the other constituents of the auxiliary - as constraints on possible trigger-target pairs.

3.1 Proximity

The ability of a speaker to use an ellipsed verb phrase, like the ability to use any kind of anaphoric expression, depends very much on the assumption that the speaker will be able to recover the particular predicate that triggered the ellipsis. That predicate is tied very closely to the exact form and lexical content of its source sentence. As many psychological experiments have shown, people only retain awareness of explicit sentences for a very short time, especially when confronted with a still continuing discourse. The result is that it is not surprising to have found no case of verb phrase ellipsis whose antecedent was further away than the preceding sentence. <*24> Therefore it will probably be adequate to confine the search space of possible antecedents to the sentence containing the ellipsed verb phrase and the sentence preceding it. (Each **sentence** may have several **clauses,** each of which can provide ellipsis triggers.)

3.2 Structural Position

There are two points about structural position which can be used to constrain a search procedure. The first derives from the fact that (1) because no sequence of terminal symbols can be identical with a proper sub-part of itself and (2) because the condition for verb phrase

---

concerning verb phrase ellipsis and stress [Janet Bing, personal communication].
<*24>. I am assuming that an ellipsed verb phrase is resolved immediately after an initial formal representation is assigned to its matrix clause (cf. Section 4). Thus given a sequence of clauses S_1, S_2, S_3, where both S_2 and S_3 are ellipsis sites, I would view S_1 as triggering the ellipsis in S_2, and S_2 (now resolved) as triggering that in S_3. I do not view S_1 as triggering both.

ellipsis - identity of predication - requires identical terminal
sequences in the logical representation (except for alphabetic
variation), it follows that (3) the predicate which triggers verb phrase
ellipsis cannot contain its target. Syntactically, this corresponds to
the observation that a full verb phrase which dominates an ellipsed one
(except for one in a non-subject relative clause, cf. Section 2.6)
cannot be the source of the latter's antecedent. Schematically, this
syntactic environment can be represented as follows, where ? indicates
the ellipsis site:

$$[_{S1}...[_{VP1}...[_{S2}...[_{VP2}?]...]...]...]$$

Unless VP2 is in a non-subject relative clause, the search space of its
possible antecedents does not include predicates which can be derived
from VP1.

The second point about structural position involves an observation
by Wasow [1972] and others that in certain relative structural
positions, an explicit verb phrase cannot be the antecedent of an
ellipsed one, even under "identity of predication". The data involved
is held to include sentences like the following. (* indicates that
according to Wasow the intended anaphor-antecedent pair cannot hold.)

36a. John tried LSD after Bill did **0**.
  b. After Bill tried LSD, John did **0**.
  c. After Bill did **0**, John tried LSD.
  d.*John did **0** after Bill tried LSD.
    0 = try LSD

37a. A man who keeps mice will usually marry a woman who does **0** too.
  b.*A man who does **0** will usually marry a woman who keeps mice too.
    0 = keeps mice

Wasow contends that if an anaphor precedes its antecedent within a
sentence, then it must also be more deeply embedded than its antecedent.
This is one version of the "backwards anaphora constraint" (BAC).
According to Wasow, example 36d. fails because a verb phrase in a
subordinate clause is more deeply embedded than that in the main clause.
Example 37b. fails because the ellipsed verb phrase hangs off a noun
phrase which both precedes and is less deeply embedded than the noun
phrase whose relative clause is the presumed source of its ellipsis
trigger.

It is not clear to me that this is such an all or none constraint
as Wasow would have it: examples 36d. and 37b. merely seem more of a
strain to resolve than the others. Nor is it clear that Wasow's is an
adequate way to state a BAC for verb phrase ellipsis (cf. [Sag, 1976]).
<*25> However there does seem to be a relative difference in the
likely location of an ellipsis trigger which a search procedure could
take advantage of, provided a syntactic representation of the current
sentence was available. (In Section 4, I shall advocate keeping around
the syntactic representation of both the current sentence and the one
preceding it.)

To close this section I want to repeat a point that Sag has made
about the dissimilarity of verb phrase ellipsis and definite pronoun
anaphora with respect to "backwards anaphora constraints", since it can
be used to reduce the computation involved in identifying possible
ellipsis triggers. For definite pronoun anaphora, a sentence is
definitely out if it fails anyone's version of BAC. For example,
    38.*He thinks John is unpopular.
is out if "he" and "John" are meant to be co-referential.

Lasnik [1976] has noted that even if sentence 38 appears in a
context where "John" is already established, e.g.

        John has problems.
        *He thinks John is unpopular.

"he" cannot be co-referential with this previous occurrence of "John".
However, Sag [1976] notes that this is not the case for verb phrase
ellipsis. That is, the antecedent of an ellipsed verb phrase can be
identical to one with which an anaphor-antecedent relation is
structurally blocked. Sag gives as examples

<*25>. BACs continue to be an area both of research and of controversy
in linguistics. So far the version that appears to parallel the data on
definite pronoun anaphora most closely is that of [Reinhart, 1976].
Reinhart dismisses the traditional "precede and command" relation in
favor of a notion of the "syntactic domain" of node A. This she defines
to be the subtree dominated by the first branching node that dominates
A. She then argues that in order for two NPs, A and B, to be
anaphorically related, where A is in the syntactic domain of B, it is
necessary that A be a pronoun. If A is not in B's syntactic domain,
there are no constraints on A's realization in order for an anaphoric
relation to hold.

```
    -Who tried LSD?
     John did 0 after Bill tried LSD.
     0 = try LSD

    -Who will try LSD?
     John will 0 if Bill tries LSD.
     0 = try LSD

    -What exists?
     A proof that God exists does 0.
     0 = exist
```

What this implies for the design of a search procedure is that not only does such an algorithm **not** have to check out a structurally blocked position for the possibility of antecedents, it does **not** have to verify that a proposed antecedent is not identical with one that is so blocked. With pronoun resolution, this second step is still necessary.

3.3 Voice Constraints

I mentioned in Section 2.1 that the subject of an ellipsed verb phrase must fill the same logical role vis a vis the ellipsis trigger as the trigger's own subject does. Because active and passive clauses differ in which logical role the surface subject fills, the two clauses involved in verb phrase ellipsis - the one with the ellipsed verb phrase and the one whose interpretation contains the ellipsis trigger - must at least have the same voice. For example,

```
    39. Wendy avoided the aardvark, and Bruce did 0 too.
        0 = avoid the aardvark

    40. The aardvark was given a nut by Wendy, and Bruce did 0 too.
        0 = ?

    41. The aardvark was given two peanuts for its birthday, and the
        axolotl was 0 too.
        0 = given two peanuts for its birthday

    42. Wendy avoided the aardvark, and the axolotl was 0 too.
        0 = ?
```

In the case of multiple passives (such as are possible with verbs which, like "give", take both a direct and an indirect object), this constraint will only be able to weed out some of the definitely inappropriate candidates, but in most other cases it is a very effective filter. <*26>

A residual problem however is though that while a remaining "do" form always signals an active voice ellipsis target, a remaining "be" form is ambiguous: it is present if the mood of the ellipsis target is progressive (example 43) or if its voice is passive (example 44) or if it is an ellipsed predicate adjective or predicate nominative (example 45).

43. Since Wendy is writing to the President, Bruce is 0 too.
    0 = writing to the President

44. The aardvark was given an apple, and the axolotl was 0 too.
    0 = given an apple

45. Bert is a super dentist and his father was 0 too.
    0 = (be) a super dentist

Moreover, it appears to me that it is often only the initial verb, and not the complete auxiliary, that remains. <#27> For example,

46. Bruce will be a legal beagle next year and Wendy will 0 too.
    (or ...and Wendy will be 0 too.)
    0 = (be) a legal beagle

47. Bruce may be given a beagle for Xmas. If not, Wendy will 0. (or
    ...Wendy will be 0.)
    0 = (be) given a beagle for Xmas

Thus a solitary remaining future, modal or "have" may be ambiguous as well, making it impossible to identify the voice of the ellipsis target and thereby constrain the search space of possible triggers on this basis.

<#26>. The one case where violations of this "same voice" constraint seem to approach acceptability involves "equi" sentences (cf. Section 2.2) in which the subject of the matrix clause and the implicit object of the embedded clause are co-referential, e.g.
    (i) Although the steaks were ready to eat at 6pm, by 7pm they still hadn't been 0.
        0 = eaten
    (ii) Usually John is easy to please, but by this play, he wasn't 0.
        0 = pleased
Here the clauses in which elision has occurred are both passive while the clauses whose interpretations contain the intended ellipsis triggers (i.e., the embedded to-complements) are active. It is not yet clear to me why such examples should approach acceptability. In the meanwhile, one can either allow a search procedure to fail in these very rare cases, or build this in as an exception.
<#27>. This may be due to subsequent elisions: according to the usual structural description of verb phrase deletion (cf. Section 1.1.), the auxiliary is not touched in the process.

3.4 Negation

An ellipsed verb phrase cannot itself be explicitly negative. <*28>
For example,

    48. Bruce didn't buy an aardvark: Wendy did **0**.
        0 = buy an aardvark, *not buy an aardvark

Thus the only way for a clause with an ellipsed verb phrase to be
understood as a negative clause when resolved is for it to contain an
explicit NEG, e.g.

        Wendy doesn't **0** either.
        Neither will **0** Wendy.
        But Wendy won't **0**.

Explicit negation (conveyed either by "not" in the clausal auxiliary or
by a negative conjunction - "neither" or "nor"), together with a
stylistic use of verb phrase ellipsis in parallel (negative/negative) or
contrastive (positive/negative) constructions, can thus be used to limit
the search for possible ellipsis triggers, as I shall now describe.

When an ellipsed verb phrase occurs in a negative clause, its
trigger is more likely to come from a positive clause if either that
clause or the negative clause contains a contrastive element. <*29>
For example,

    49. Although Bruce can spend hours at The Byte Shop, Wendy can't **0**.
        0 = spend hours at The Byte Shop

On the other hand, its trigger is more likely to come from a negative
clause if its own clause contains a parallel element like "either" or
"neither".

    50. A man who doesn't smoke can play volley ball for hours.
        Moreover, he can go out with a woman who doesn't **0** either.
        0 = smoke, *play volley ball for hours

"Too" cannot normally be used as a parallel element in a negative
context, e.g.

<*28>. Standard transformational linguistics holds NEG to be part of
the sentential auxiliary and not part of the verb phrase. Thus NEG will
not be removed by verb phrase ellipsis.
<*29>. This may be as explicit as a word like "but" or "although", or
it may be part of the stress pattern of the utterance, which in written
text must be re-constructed from its semantics. In the latter case,
negation can no longer be used as a **simple** constraint on possible
antecedents.

*John doesn't 0 too.

Thus if "too" does appear following an ellipsed verb phrase it rules out a negative trigger, e.g.

    51. John doesn't like Mary.
      *Fred does 0 too.
      0 = *like Mary, *not like Mary

3.5 Tense and Aspect

The other types of information besides voice and negation which are contained in the clausal auxiliary (and will therefore not be removed by verb phrase ellipsis) are tense, mood (e.g. progressive, perfective) and modality (e.g. "can", "must", "may", etc.). None of these provides as strong a constraint on possible ellipsis triggers as does voice because they do not change role assignments. The result is that neither tense, mood nor modality must be preserved across a trigger-target pair, cf.

    52. If Bruce ate corn flakes yesterday, do you think he will 0 today?
      0 = eat corn flakes

    53. I know I can eat corn flakes, but must I 0?
      0 = eat corn flakes

    54. No one can stop me from eating corn flakes, although Bruce has tried to 0.
      0 = stop me from eating corn flakes

    55. Just because I have eaten corn flakes doesn't mean that I want to 0.
      0 = eat cornflakes

4. Resolving Verb Phrase Ellipsis

In this section, I shall elaborate on the framework for discourse model synthesis and definite anaphor resolution presented in Chapter 2 and discuss ellipsis resolution in the context of producing the Level-2 semantic interpretation of a sentence. The two problem areas I will concentrate on are (1) the order in which to process ellipsed verb phrases if several should occur in one sentence and (2) the order in which to process ellipsed verb phrases vis a vis definite pronouns.

Let me briefly review that framework. I am assuming that as a sentence comes into the system, it is labelled according to its sequential place in the discourse and parsed into a surface structure parse tree. That parse tree (or if the sentence is structurally ambiguous, each distinct parse tree) is then passed to an interpreter to determine its Level-1 representation. (If a parse tree cannot be so interpreted, it will be discarded.) Each distinct Level-1 representation is then passed to a second interpreter that attempts to produce a Level-2 semantic interpretation in which, **inter alia**, ellipsed verb phrases and definite anaphora have been resolved. That Level-2 interpretation is then processed for the new discourse entities it evokes, possibly resulting in **referential** Level-2 interpretations as well.

The first additional assumption I am making is that each S node in the parse tree (matrix and embedded) is tagged with its Level-2 interpretation in the subject/predicate format specified in Section 2.1. (If the subject of the S is an existential, this should be the referential Level-2 interpretation, cf. Section 2.3.) <*30>   For example,

56. Bruce wanted to buy Wendy an aardvark.

```
S NP NPR Bruce
  AUX TENSE past
      VOICE active
  VP V want
     NP S NP ***
          AUX VOICE active
          VP V buy
             NP NPR Wendy
             NP DET ART a
                NOM N aardvark
                NU singular
```

$[S_{56}$ INTERP Bruce, $\lambda(r)[W\ r,\{r, \lambda(s)[(Ey:A)\ .\ B\ s,y,e_5]\}]]$

$[S_{56.1}$ INTERP r, $\lambda(s)[(Ey:A)\ .\ B\ s,y,e_5]]$

(*** stands for the subject of the to-complement, which is co-referential with the subject of the matrix. **W** stands for "wanted" and **B** for "bought". e_5 is assumed to be the label of the discourse

---

<*30>. This tagging is separate from the procedure I described in Chapter 2, Section 6, whereby every interpretation is tagged with the set of discourse entities associated with it.

entity evoked by "Wendy".) The reason for producing a tagged parse tree
is to enable the search for possible sources of the ellipsis trigger to
be carried out at a syntactic level, where several effective search
constraints can be stated very simply (cf. Section 3).   Whenever a
clause (i.e., an S node) is identified as a possible source, its
interpretation can then be picked off that node via the tag.   The
ellipsis triggers associated with that interpretation include not only
its explicit predicate, but other ones derivable according to procedures
motivated in Section 2. (In Section 5, I will make an initial attempt
to characterize some other special but necessary procedures.) I am
assuming that the search for acceptable trigger sites will be carried on
through both the sentence containing the ellipsis and the one preceding
it. (Further back than that is extremely, cf. Section 3.1.) Thus I am
assuming that parse trees will not be discarded immediately, but will be
available until at least one more sentence has been processed.

     I shall now consider what happens when a sentence with one or more
ellipsed verb phrases is encountered. After it is labelled and parsed,
<*31> its parse tree will be assigned an Level-1 semantic
interpretation in which its ellipsed verb phrase(s) have not yet been
resolved. (I am using **P?** to indicate an unresolved predicate.)   There
are at least two reasons for not attempting to resolve the ellipsed verb
phrase(s) during this first interpretation phase: (1) the ellipsis
trigger may follow the ellipsis site (Section 3.2) or (2) in the case of
ellipsis from non-subject relative clauses, the ellipsis trigger may
span the ellipsis site (Section 2.6). An attempt to resolve ellipsed
verb phrase(s) is made during the second interpretation phase.

     The question arises of what order to follow in resolving multiple
instances of verb phrase ellipsis within the same sentence. The problem
is that there is no way to avoid the possibility that the intuitively
correct trigger for one instance of ellipsis may contain an embedded
predicate that may itself undergo subsequent elision under identity with
some other predicate.   To see this, consider the following sentence
pairs.

<*31>. A special symbol like **0** or **?** will appear in the parse tree in

57a. Has Wendy travelled around Nepal yet?
  b. No. And although she claims she doesn't 0_1, I know she really
     wants to 0_2.
     0_1 = want to travel around Nepal
     0_2 = travel around Nepal

58a. Has Wendy travelled around Nepal yet?
  b. No. And although she claims she doesn't want to 0_1, I know she
     really does 0_2.
     0_1 = travel around Nepal
     0_2 = want to travel around Nepal

Recall from Section 3.2 that the trigger for a given instance of verb
phrase ellipsis may be found either anywhere to its left or else to its
right in a less deeply embedded clause. Thus if the ellipses in a
sentence are processed left-to-right, then in sentence 57b. the possible
antecedents for 0_1 would be found to be

  (a) travel around Nepal (from sentence 57a.)
  (b) know she really wants to 0_2
  (c) want to 0_2

where 0_2 would have not yet been resolved. On the other hand, if the
multiple ellipses in a sentence are processed starting from the least
deeply embedded one, then in sentence 58b. the possible antecedents for
0_2 would be found to be

  (a) travel around Nepal (from sentence 58a.)
  (b) claim she doesn't want to 0_1
  (c) want to 0_1

where in this case 0_1 would have not yet been resolved.

Since this situation cannot be avoided by choosing either
left-to-right or "shallow-to-deep" processing, a possible solution would
seem to be to permit the resolution of a leftward-lying (or less deeply
embedded) ellipsed verb phrase to be interrupted, pending resolution of
an ellipsed verb phrase to its right (or below it) which has been
identified as a potential trigger site. If this solution is adopted,
experience will show whether there would ever be more than one such
interrupted process at any one time.

The other question that arises is that of the order in which
ellipsed verb phrases should be resolved vis a vis definite anaphora.
The answer seems to be that an ellipsed verb phrase should be resolved

place of each ellipsed verb phrase.

before a definite anaphor, since it is possible for the latter to refer to a discourse entity or parameterized individual evoked by the ellipsed verb phrase. For example,

> 59a. Where would someone who owns an aardvark keep it?
>   b. Well, one girl who does **0** keeps **it** in the kitchen.
>   0 = owns an aardvark
>   it = the just-mentioned aardvark she owns

> 60a. John didn't bake a cake for Wendy.
>   b. On the other hand, Bruce did **0**, but she didn't like **it**.
>   0 = bake a cake for Wendy
>   it = the just-mentioned cake that Bruce baked for Wendy

In both of these examples, if the ellipsed verb phrase has not yet been resolved, there is no way of accounting for the referents of the subsequent pronouns. In fact, linguists have used the term "missing antecedent" [Grinder & Postal, 1971] to describe any situation in which the "antecedent" of a definite pronoun is not explicit, being somehow "contained" in an ellipsed constituent, as in the preceding two examples.

It should be obvious though that with the treatment of definite anaphora and verb phrase ellipsis presented here, there is no such thing as a "missing antecedent": it is merely a matter of the order in which anaphoric expressions are resolved.

Let us consider the processing of example 60 in detail. Following parsing and both phases of semantic interpretation, the following Level-2 representation would be produced for sentence 60a.

$$\sim \text{John, } \lambda(r)[(Ex:Cake) \text{ . Bake } r,x,Wendy]$$

Because this formula is negated, the existential is not immediately assumed to evoke a discourse entity (Chapter 2, Section 5.4). Next, following parsing and the first phase of semantic interpretation, the following Level-1 representation would be produced for sentence 60b.

$$P? \text{ Bruce \& } \sim \text{SHE, } \lambda(s)[\text{Like } s,IT]$$

Taking this clause by clause, one plausible antecedent for P? is the unary predicate in the preceding sentence. Resolving P? in this way yields

$$\text{Bruce, } \lambda(r)[(Ex:Cake) \text{ . Bake } r,x,Wendy]$$

i.e., "Bruce baked a cake for Wendy". The existential term, no longer within the scope of negation, can be seen now to evoke a discourse entity (say e_{60}) describable as

ix: Cake x & Bruce, $\lambda(r)$[Bake r,x,Wendy] & **evoke** S_{60a},x

i.e., "the just-mentioned cake that Bruce baked for Wendy". This in turn is a plausible referent for IT in the second clause, Wendy being a plausible referent for SHE. That is,

... & ~ PRO=Wendy, $\lambda(s)$[Like s, PRO=e_{60}]

in this approach, "missing antecedents" are only missing in the surface sentence: they are not missing in the underlying formal representation once the ellipsed verb phrase has been resolved.

5. Inference and Verb Phrase Ellipsis

I mentioned in Section 1.1 that one deficiency in Sag's strict logical form approach to verb phrase ellipsis lies in its inability to account for examples in which the intuitively correct ellipsis trigger is not an explicit constituent of "logical form". Thus far it is a deficiency in the current account as well. Such examples seem to require allowing people to use as ellipsis triggers predicates associated with a limited class of inferable propositions. The problem is both to justify that view and then to characterize that class.

For justification, I call on the fact that the process of constructing a formal representation of a sentence is part of the normal process of understanding discourse. Given this, it is possible that **alternative** ways of understanding a sentence or sequence of sentences or even valid. salient **implications** of sentences may also provide usable triggers for verb phrase ellipsis. So whereas Sag's approach implies a very **static** view of verb phrase ellipsis, the above process-oriented view suggests that a more **plastic** approach is justified.

Now "alternative ways of understanding" and "valid implications" are both notions which involve inference. But not every valid inference provides lambda-predicates accessible to verb phrase ellipsis. For example, the following axiom relates the notions of "selling" and "being bought".

(∀x)(∀y)(∀z) . x, λ(r)[r sold y to z] ==>
   y, λ(s)[s was bought by z]

i.e., if any x sold any y to any z, then y was bought by z". Notice
that this axiom is not sufficient to produce a predicate "was bought by
z", given an explicit predicate "sold y to z" --

    61. Bruce sold a waffle iron to Wendy, and an electric wok was **0**
       too.
       0 ≠ bought by Wendy

    Unfortunately, aside from the caveat that the logical forms of both
the overt sentence(s) and the derived one be "similar" in some undefined
sense, there seem to be no hard and fast rules delimiting the class of
productive inferences relative to verb phrase ellipsis. What I shall do
in this section then is to set down some inference schemata which
account for some otherwise problematic examples of verb phrase ellipsis.

5.1 Conjoined Predicates and 'Headless' Relatives

    Conjunction, of one sort or another, seems to be involved in two of
the cases I have noticed where the predicate which has triggered verb
phrase ellipsis is not an explicit constituent. As a first example,
consider:

    62a. I can walk and I can chew gum.
      b. Gerry can **0** too, but not at the same time.
      0 = walk and chew gum

In order to account for such examples, one can postulate a rule schema
which conjoins a sequence of propositions with identical subjects and
abstracts a new predicate off the common argument, i.e.,

    [RW-2] y, λ(r)[**P** r] & y, λ(s)[**Q** s] ==> y, λ(t)[**P** t & **Q** t]

Informally this says that if y **P**'s and y **Q**'s, then y **P**'s and **Q**'s. The
propositions on either side of the implication ("==>"), while
structurally different, are semantically equivalent (at least with
respect to an extensional semantics).

    To illustrate the application of this inference schema, consider a
representation of sentence 62a.

       I, λ(r)[Walk r] & I, λ(s)[Chew s, "gum"]

Since this matches the left-hand side of the above rule schema, it
follows that

I, $\lambda(r)$[Walk r & Chew r, "gum"]

Intuitively this predicate, paraphrasable as "walk and chew gum", is what has triggered the elision in sentence 62b. <*32>

The other case that I want to consider here illustrates the need for a rule schema that can be applied to a sequence of propositions with non-identical subjects. Consider the following examples.

63. Wendy is eager to sail around the world and Bruce is eager to climb Kilimanjaro, but neither of them can **0** because money is too tight.
    0 = do what s/he is eager to do

64. Each fifth-grade boy wants to sail around the world and each fifth-grade girl wants to climb Kilimanjaro. However, I fear that none of them ever will **0**.
    0 = do what s/he wants to do

65. Bruce promised to eat his spinach and Wendy promised to throw hers at the cat, but neither of them did **0** because they were served green beans instead.
    0 = do what s/he promised to do

66. Since Bruce was given the chance to climb Kilimanjaro and Wendy was given the chance to sail to Tahiti, each of them did **0**.
    0 = do what s/he was given the chance to do

In each case, the ellipsed verb phrase appears with a distributively quantified plural subject - i.e.,

negative: $(\forall x \in THEY)$. $\sim x, \lambda(r)[P? \ r]$
positive: $(\forall x \in THEY)$. $x, \lambda(r)[P? \ r]$

(The former is the unambiguous logical interpretation of any clause containing the phrase "neither of them" or "none of them".)

<*32>. One special restriction here is that the conjuncts must have identical auxiliaries. (Identity can be verified against the syntactic representation of the clauses, cf. Section 4.) This permits an interpretation in which the activities conveyed by the predicates can be taken as simultaneous. (The predicates themselves don't really imply anything about time.) Examples with non-identical auxiliaries sound very strange, for example,

John attended Harvard, and now he is going to MIT.
Fred {did, does, will, is} **0** too.

"Fred did **0** too" seems to imply only that he attended Harvard. "Fred is **0** too" seems to imply only that he is now going to MIT. The other auxiliaries just seem bizarre. The sense that Fred also attended Harvard and is now going to MIT does not seem to be conveyable using an ellipsed verb phrase.

What I suggest is that one potential antecedent for an ellipsed verb phrase can be derived by some "logical form" correlate of "headless" relatives [Hankamer 1974]. For example, sentence 63 can be paraphrased in the following "headless" relative form

63'. What Wendy is eager to do is to sail around the world and what Bruce is eager to do is to climb Kilimanjaro, but neither of them can **0** because money is too tight.

From this, it is simple to infer the almost tautologous form

66''. Wendy is eager to do what she is eager to do and Bruce is eager to do what he is eager to do, but neither of them can **0** because money is too tight.

In this form, however, where the same thing is predicated of both Wendy and Bruce, the ellipsed verb phrase can indeed be seen to have a simple explicit trigger - i.e., "do what s/he is eager to do". The same paraphrasing and inferencing pattern will produce the intuitively correct trigger in each of the other examples as well.

While I am not yet sure how to express what is involved here in terms of the Level-2 semantic interpretations on which it will operate, the important thing to note is that it is only structural patterns and not world knowledge which is involved in the derivation of these non-explicit ellipsis triggers.

5.2 Split Reciprocals

In the next set of examples, the antecedent for the ellipsed verb phrase can be interpreted synonymously with one of the two sides of an explicit **reciprocal** verb phrase. To make this clearer, consider the following sentences

67. Irv and Martha wanted to dance together, but Martha's mother said that she couldn't **0**.
    0 = dance with Irv

68. Irv and Martha wanted to dance with each other, but Martha's mother said that she couldn't **0**.
    0 = dance with Irv

Both of the explicit verb phrases which give rise to these antecedents express a reciprocal activity, i.e. "dance together" and "dance with each other". The ellipsed verb phrases seem related to these by conveying the sense of one side of the interaction.

A very simple, first-pass approach to this would be to associate with "together", "each other" and other reciprocals information to the effect that if <a> and<b> do <P> together (or with each other, etc.), then <a> does <P> with <b> and <b> does <P> with <a>. This schematic information would be accessible in identifying possible ellipsis triggers. For example, from the consequent clause of either 67 or 68 above, the one-place predicates

$\lambda(r)$[Dance r, Irv]   and $\lambda(s)$[Dance s, Martha]

i.e. "dancing with Irv" and "dancing with Martha", would be available as possible ellipsis triggers. With "Martha" presumably the subject of Martha's mother's prohibition, the former is the only one permitted by case agreement in these examples.

5.3 Embedded Descriptions

The final set of examples that I want to consider here was suggested to me by a discussion of "do so" anaphora in [Kaplan, 1976].

    69. The country that Joe wants to visit is China, and he will 0 too,
        if he gets an invitation there soon.
        0 = visit China

    70. China is a country that Joe wants to visit, and he will 0 too,
        if he gets an invitation there soon.
        0 = visit China

The reasoning involved in identifying "visit China" as the intended ellipsis trigger in both cases seems to be that if China is either the country or a country that Joe wants to visit, then Joe wants to visit China. The definite case can be stated more generally as

    [RW-3] ix: $\lambda(u:C)$[P a,u]x = b   ==> a, $\lambda(r)$[P r,b]

and the indefinite case, as

    [RW-4] $\lambda(u:C)$[P a,u] b   ==> a, $\lambda(r)$[P r,b]

The suggestion is that the predicate of the consequent clause in either case is a viable ellipsis trigger.

The initial clauses of examples 69 and 70 can be represented as

    ix: $\lambda(u:C)$[Joe, $\lambda(r)$[Want r, {r, $\lambda(s)$[Visit s,u]}]] = China

and

    $\lambda(u:C)$[Joe, $\lambda(r)$[Want r, {r, $\lambda(s)$[Visit s,u]}]] China

respectively, where C stands for "country". Applying the appropriate
rule schema - RW-3 in the first case, RW-4 in the second - leads to the
same expression in both cases, namely

      Joe, λ(r)[Want r, {r, λ(s)[Visit s,China}]

i.e., "Joe wants to visit China". This contains two unary predicates
which are available as possible ellipsis triggers, namely

- λ(r)[Want r, {r, λ(s)[Visit s, China}]
  "wanting to visit China"
- λ(s)[Visit s, China]
  "visiting China"

In both examples 69 and 70, the latter is the intuitively correct
antecedent for pragmatic reasons.

    As I meant to convey in the introduction to this section, verb
phrase ellipsis is not a closed book.   Instances of ellipsed verb
phrases will probably continue to appear whose antecedents must be
explained in other ways than with recourse to the admittedly tentative
rule schemas presented here. Moreover, there are bound to be pragmatic
constraints on their applicability which I haven't even considered. On
this note, it is fitting to conclude the chapter, reviewing what
essentially has been presented here.

6. Summary

    To summarize the main points of this chapter, I have done the
following things:

1. I have shown that recent claims that verb phrase ellipsis is
   conditioned by "identity of predication" at the level of
   "logical form" are only tenable if one drops the notion that a
   sentence has a single correct "logical form": alternative
   formal views of a sentence lead to alternative ellipsis
   triggers.

2. I have characterized various formal ways that sentences must
   be viewed and represented in order to maintain an "identity of
   predication" account (Section 2).

3. I have shown that (for at least the classes of sentences I
   have considered) a sentence can be assigned a single
   representation to which simple procedures can be applied, when
   desirable, to produce other appropriate representations.

4. I have shown the value of using both syntactic and formal
   representations in handling verb phrase ellipsis - the former

to constrain possible trigger sites (Section 3), the latter from which to derive possible triggers (Section 2).

5. I have shown how resolving verb phrase ellipsis can and must be integrated with resolving definite anaphora (Section 4).

6. I think I have shown that no account of possible ellipsis triggers can be complete without bringing in the notion of inference (Section 5).

TABLE OF CONTENTS

CHAPTER 5. Conclusion

1. Summary

In the first chapter of this thesis, I made two strong claims about the task of identifying what a text makes available for anaphoric reference.

1. None of the three types of anaphoric expressions that I have studied - definite anaphora, "one"-anaphora and verb phrase ellipsis - can be understood in purely linguistic terms. That is, none of them can be explained without stepping out of the language into the conceptual model each participant is synthesizing from the discourse.

2. On the other hand, if a discourse participant does not assign to each new utterance in the discourse a formal representation in which, **inter alia,**
   a. quantifiers are indicated, along with their scopes;
   b. main clauses are distinguished from relative clauses and subordinate clauses
   c. clausal subjects are separated from clausal predicates;
   then s/he will not be able to identify all of what is being made available for anaphoric reference.

Chapters 2-4 contain the evidence which led me to made these claims, as well as a discussion of their implications for natural language man/machine communication. Throughout these chapters, I stress the importance of descriptions and the ability to form appropriate ones from the text. What I want to stress finally is the computational and linguistic value of studying several types of anaphora at once. It has enabled me to see possible solutions to problematic cases in linguistics and to design what I hope will be a robust procedure for handling three types of anaphora that will not collapse into a twitching heap when asked to handle a fourth.

2. Future Research

Although implementation always reveals interesting problems which are hidden to gedanken research, my current curiousity lies in the following three areas: (1) integrating data-driven aspects of model synthesis such as were discussed here and expectation-driven aspects, often discussed in the context of "frames", "scripts", etc.;

(2) identifying the reference requirements of limited contexts; and (3) exploring anaphoric reference to discourse entities evoked by sentences and larger units of text. While I haven't pursued any of these topics systematically as yet, the following remarks might serve to explain my interest in them.

2.1 Data-driven and Expectation-driven Processes in Model Synthesis

In this thesis, my basic viewpoint has been bottom up - identifying the discourse entities that come from the explicit text and the way they arise. I have looked at discourse entities both as inhabitants of the speaker's model of the situation s/he is trying to communicate and as inhabitants of the listener's model s/he is simultaneously trying to synthesize. It is these discourse entities, and not things in the text or "out there", that are referenced by definite anaphora.

Now there is another line of AI research that talks in terms of the listener's model of the discourse. Its concern is **inference** in text understanding - trying to account for a listener's ability to fill in aspects of the underlying situation that have not been made explicit in the text, to answer questions about that situation, even to ask questions about it, etc.

Collins, Brown & Larkin [1977] characterize two approaches to inference in text understanding: "text-based" and "model-based". The text-based view

> "...stresses the notion that the inference process looks for meaningful relations between different propositions in the text." [Collins, Brown & Larkin, 1977:2]

It characterizes the approach taken by Charniak [1972], Hobbs [1976a&b] and Rieger [1975]. The model-based view, on the other hand,

> "...argues that a central purpose of inference is to synthesize an underlying model which organizes and augments the surface structure fragments in the text. In this view, inference is controlled by a target structure that specifies the **a priori** constraints on the kind of model to be synthesized. This target structure acts as an organizational principle for guiding a set of inference procedures." [Collins, Brown & Larkin, 1977:2]

Such a model-based approach to inference characterizes recent work by Bullwinkle [1977], Lehnert [1977], Rumelhart & Ortony [1977] and Schank & Abelson [1975].

By far the most interesting version of this approach is that of Collins, Brown & Larkin [1977] themselves. According to them,

> "...text understanding proceeds by progressive refinement from an initial model to more and more refined models of the text. The target structure guides the construction process, constraining the models to the class of well-formed, goal-subgoal structures that **means-ends analysis** [Newell & Simon 1963] produces. The initial model is an partial model, constructed from schemas triggered by the beginning elements of the text. Successive models incorporate more and more elements from the text. The models are progressively refined by trying to fill the unspecified variable slots in each model as it is constructed." [Collins, Brown & Larkin 1977:4-5]

Since this intuitively seems to be the appropriate way to view text understanding, it raises several questions for my own line of research. Among them are the following:

(1) Does it still make sense to view the text as **evoking** discourse entities in the way I have presented?

(2) How do these entities relate to what is, in some sense, "already there" in the partial model?

(3) How important are the discourse entity descriptions (**IDs**) derived from the explicit text? What role do they play in model synthesis and refinement?

(4) Can this view of text understanding as progressive model synthesis provide a way to account for people's ability to ignore most of the large number of discourse entities that unconstrained ID-rule application seems capable of producing?

In the long run, it is probable that studying the integration of data-driven and expectation-driven aspects of model synthesis will have as much relevance for basic education - especially reading - as for natural language man/machine communication.

2.2 Reference Requirements in Limited Contexts

The issue of reference in limited contexts arises when one considers a limited task and/or limited topic natural language understanding system such as the ones that have been constructed to date. The question is whether such systems actually need the full range of reference handling abilities used by people engaged in normal unconstrained human discourse and documented, in part, in the previous chapters. Might they not be freed from the need for certain abilities by either their limited world views or the limited tasks they are engaged in? Can not some generalizations be made about the demands of reference handling in limited contexts?

It is an interesting issue whose solution is of potential benefit for the design of efficient and effective natural language front-ends. One aspect of this issue is the question of whether there are circumstances which would free a system from the need to deal with discourse entities in terms of their **IDs** and enable it to deal directly with them in terms of unique names. For example, consider the sequence

    1a. Snow White saw some dwarfs walking through the woods.
     b. She called to **them**, but **they** didn't seem to hear her.

The question is whether there are circumstances in which a system would not have to derive a description like "the just-mentioned set of dwarfs that Snow White saw walking through the woods", would not have to attach it as a defining property to some new discourse entity, and would not have to use that description to identify that entity as a possible referent for "they" and "them" in the next sentence. Are there circumstances in which it could deal directly with the particular set {Dopey Sneezy Bashful Grumpy etc.}?

I should point out here that even if there are circumstances which free a system from the need to derive and manipulate discourse entity **IDs**, it must still be able to recognize all the entities that the discourse can evoke. That is, a question like

    2a. Did every new student bring a dog?

if answered in the affirmative, can naturally be followed by

    2b. Have **they** all been inspected for rabies?

In some form or another, the correct referent for "them" (i.e., not the set of new students) must be available, whether it be as a set entity {Rover Tchaik Damp-Stanley ...} or the individual entity describable as "the just-mentioned set of dogs, each of which was brought by some new student."

While I have not considered this question carefully, it seems to me that a minimal requirement is that the system presumes to know all the properties of every element (i.e., individual and set) in its domain. (The number of such elements need not, I think, be finite, just as long as the system assumes that it can determine all the properties of each element.) Clearly if a system does not make this assumption (akin to the "closed world" assumption for data bases discussed in [Reiter, 1977]), then it must be able to derive and manipulate IDs.

For example, this assumption was not made in the Travel Budget Manager's Assistant system developed at BBN as part of the Speech Understanding Project [Woods et al., 1975]. If this system were told "Two people from the Speech Group are going to the ASA meeting in November", it could not assume that it would find the names of (i.e., unique labels for) those two individuals in its data base. Thus if it were to be able to deal with subsequent references to that set, it would have to have been in terms of a discourse entity describable as "the just-mentioned two people from the Speech Group who are going to the ASA meeting in November".

On the other hand, the LUNAR system developed at BBN for NASA's Lunar Receiving Laboratory [Woods et al. 1972] did presume to know all the properties of each element in its domain (set, as well as individual). Thus if it were asked "Are there any analyses of a breccia for chromium?", it could answer the question with a list of specific analyses and then deal with subsequent references to that set in terms of the explicit list. It did not have to derive a discourse entity ID like "the just-mentioned analyses of some breccia for chromium". That in many cases LUNAR did deal in terms of IDs was because the alternative (given the more than 13,000 separate analyses it knew about) could involve a great expense in computation and storage.

I am sure that many factors are involved in determining the reference requirements of limited systems, including what a system's activities are (e.g. question-answering, information acquisition, etc.), whether the user's view of the system and the system's view of itself agree, etc. I am also sure that the results of research in this area

will be of extreme benefit to the development of competant and practical
natural language man/machine communication.

2.3 Sententially-evoked Discourse Entities

   The issue of characterizing the type of discourse entity evoked by
a sentence or larger unit of text arises when one considers what it is
that the definite pronoun "it" refers to in each of the following
continuations of sentence 3.

   3. Bruce played the Moonlight Sonata for three days.

   4a. **It** led to his being evicted from his apartment.
       it =? the event lasting three days during which Bruce
             repeatedly played the Moonlight Sonata.

    b. Each time he **did it**$_1$, **it**$_2$ got worse.
       did it$_1$ =? engaged in the act of playing the Moonlight
                Sonata once
       it$_2$ =? the quality of that act of playing of the
                Moonlight Sonata

    c. While he was **doing it,** Wendy fed him quarts of Gatorade.
       doing it =? engaging in the activity of playing the
                Moonlight Sonata repeatedly

    d. Marcia didn't believe **it.**
       it =? the assertion that sentence 3 was a correct way to
             describe reality

   These tentative descriptions of the referents of "it" each involve
one of the terms "event", "act", "process", "performance", "assertion"
and "activity". These, together with various other terms (e.g. "task",
"achievement", "accomplishment", "state", "situation", etc.), have been
used in the philosophy, AI, psychology and linguistics literatures to
classify ways of describing chunks of space-time and what can happen
during such a chunk (cf. Bach [forthcoming], Dowty [1972], Mourelatos
[1978], Norman & Rumelhart [1975], Steedman [1977], and Vendler [1967]).
One goal of this research appears to be a systematization of the valid
inferences that can be drawn from a given sentence. If, for example, a
sentence is taken to express an "activity" (i.e., a happening occupying
a period of time [Vendler, 1967]), then that activity can also be
truthfully ascribed to any sub-stretch of that period.   More
specifically, both Vendler and Steedman would classify sentence 5 below
as expressing an activity

5. Wendy has been running for an hour.

Thus it would be correct to infer from it that Wendy has been running for every time stretch within that hour.

Now one general assumption of all this research on classifying descriptions of spatio-temporal chunks is that the class to which a sentence belongs <*1> and thus the set of inferences that may validly be drawn from it can be determined by such things as the main verb of the sentence, its tense and aspect and the presence of certain types of temporal adverbs. For example, Steedman classifies the sentence

6. The program ran in 2.3 seconds.

as an "accomplishment" (i.e., a happening over a time period which has some intrinsic conclusion [Vendler, 1967]) based on the presence of the adverbial "in 2.3 seconds" and on his view that the more basic sentence - "The program ran" - expresses an activity. In the progressive mood or with a temporal adverbial like "for an hour", the sentence would also be classified as an "activity".

7. The program is running.
8. The program ran for an hour.

Returning now to example 3, Steedman would classify the more basic sentence to which it seems related

9. Bruce played the Moonlight Sonata.

as an accomplishment. The addition of the "for" time adverbial in example 3

3. Bruce played the Moonlight Sonata for three days.

would cause the latter sentence to be classified as an activity, one involving the continual repetition of the basic accomplishment expressed in sentence 9 above.

The problem regarding reference is that no matter how a sentence is classified - as expressing a state, an accomplishment, an activity, etc. - what becomes accessible anaphorically (to even the semantically empty pronoun "it") includes phenomena which would themselves be classified differently. So while sentence 3 expresses an activity, what is

---

<*1>. Each author has a slightly different typology. I will be following Vendler and Steedman here to illustrate my points.

accessible anaphorically is not only that activity (4c.) but an accomplishment (4a.) - i.e., something with an intrinsic end, the end of that three day period, the set of individual accomplishments (4b.), and an assertion (4d.) as well. In a similar vein, while sentence 10 expresses an "achievement" (i.e., an instantaneous occurrence [Vendler, 1967]), what is accessible anaphorically includes not only that specific event (11a.) but an abstracted event (11b.), an assertion (11c.) and even a time period (11d.). <*2>

10. Wendy tripped on a banana peel yesterday.

11a. **It** happened at 2:03pm right outside the monkey house.
    it = that specific event

b. And **it** happened to me today.
    it = an event of tripping on a banana peel

c. But Bruce refused to believe **it**.
    it = that that assertion is a true description of reality

d. While she was falling, she swore off zoos.
    while she was falling = the time between being upright and
                            being prone in that tripping event

My feeling is that in order to deal with what it is that sentences, paragraphs and larger units of text can make accessible anaphorically, the simple view of discourse entities presented earlier will have to be extended to a more complex view of them as multi-faceted, highly structured objects. This will allow the discourse model itself (as well as subparts of it) to be viewed as discourse entities. Then it can be shown how the facet expressed when a discourse entity is evoked is only one of several that can be ascribed to it and that can be accessed anaphorically. That "structured objects" is the direction in which AI research on representations of knowledge is now moving (cf. Bobrow & Winograd [1977]; Brachman [1978]; Smith [1978]; Woods & Brachman [1978]) should be of great benefit to future research in this area.

<*2>. While I am not sure whether the time period could be accessed with a definite pronoun, this example shows that it can certainly be accessed by a definite adverbial.

3. Epilogue

In this thesis I have tried to characterize the basic demands that handling normal human use of anaphoric expressions can make on a natural language understanding system.   I have focused on the notion of a discourse model and necessary aspects of its synthesis from the text.   I have tried to show the symbiotic relationship between discourse model construction and anaphor resolution.   There are many threads that have been left hanging, and an implementation is waiting in the wings.   It is now time to begin.

* * * FINIS * * *

Bibliography

Akmajian, A. & Jackendoff, R. Coreferentiality and Stress. **Linguistic Inquiry**, 1970, **1**(1), 124-126.

Bach, E. **Topics in English Metaphysics.** Chapter 1. (Draft of forthcoming book).

Balzer, R., Goldman, N. & Wile, D. Informality in Program Specifications. **Proceedings of 5-IJCAI**, 22-25 August 1977, 389-397.

Bartsch, R. Syntax and Semantics of Relative Clauses. In R. Bartsch, J. Groenendijk & M. Stokhof (Eds.), **Amsterdam Papers on Formal Grammars.** The Netherlands: University of Amsterdam, 1976.

Bates, M. & Bobrow, R. RUS. Forthcoming BBN Report . Cambridge MA: Bolt Beranek and Newman Inc., 1978.

Bobrow, D.G. & Winograd, T. An Overview of KRL, a Knowledge Representation Language. **Cognitive Science**, 1977, **1**(1), 3-46.

Brachman, R. A Structural Paradigm for Representing Knowledge. (BBN Report 3605). Cambridge MA: Bolt Beranek and Newman Inc., 1978.)

Bresnan, J. A Note on the Notion "Identity of Sense Anaphora". **Linguistic Inquiry**, 1971, **2**(4), 589-597.

Bresnan, J. A Realistic Transformational Grammar. In M. Halle, J. Bresnan & G. Miller (Eds.), **Linguistic Theory and Psychological Reality.** Cambridge MA: The MIT Press, 1978.

Brown, J.S. & Burton, R.R. Multiple Representations of Knowledge for Tutorial Reasoning. In D. Bobrow & A. Collins (Eds.), **Representation & Understanding.** New York: Academic Press, 1975.

Bullwinkle, C. Levels of Complexity for Anaphora Disambiguation and Speech Act Interpretation. **Proceedings of 5-IJCAI**, 22-25 August 1977, 43-49.

Burton, R. **Semantic Grammar: an engineering technique for constructing natural language understanding systems.** (BBN Report No. 3433). Cambridge MA: Bolt Beranek and Newman Inc., 1976.

Caramazza, A., Grober, E., Garvey, C. & Yates, J. Comprehension of Anaphoric Pronouns. **J. of Verbal Learning and Verbal Behavior**, 1977, **16**, 601-609.

Chafe, W. Language and Consciousness. **Language**, 1974, **50**(1), 111-133.

Chafe, W. Givenness, Contrastiveness, Definiteness, Subjects, Topics and Points of View. In C. Li (Ed.), **Subject and Topic.** New York: Academic Press, 1976.

Charniak, E. Towards a Model of Children's Story Comprehension. (Technical Report 266) MIT Artificial Intelligence Laboratory, MIT, Cambridge MA, 1972.

Charniak, E. Organization and Inference in a Frame-like System of Common Knowledge. In B. Nash-Webber & R. Schank (Eds.), **Theoretical Issues in Natural Language Processing** - Workshop proceedings. Cambridge MA, 1975.

Chomsky, N. **Aspects of the Theory of Syntax**. Cambridge MA: MIT Press, 1965.

Chomsky, N. **Reflections on Language**. New York: Pantheon Books, 1975a.

Chomsky, N. Conditions on Rules of Grammar. Unpublished ms., Department of Linguistics, MIT, 1975b.

Church, A. **The Calculi of Lambda Conversion**. Princeton NJ: Princeton University Press, 1941.

Collins, A., Brown, J.S. and Larkin, K. Inference in Text Understanding. (CSR-40) Center for the Study of Reading, U. of Illinois and Bolt Beranek and Newman Inc., 1977. (Also in R. Spiro, B. Bruce and W. Brewer (Eds.), **Theoretical Issues in Reading Comprehension**. New Jersey: Lawrence Erlbaum Associates, 1978.)

Culicover, P. A Constraint on Coreferentiality. **Foundations of Language**, 1976, 14(1).

Donnellan, K. Reference and Definite Descriptions. **The Philosophical Review**, 1966, **75**, 281-304.

Dowty, D.R. **Studies in the Logic of Verb Aspect and Time Reference in English**. Unpublished doctoral dissertation. Department of Linguistics, University of Texas at Austin, 1972.

Edmonson, J.A. Semantics, Games and Anaphoric Chains. In R. Bartsch, J. Groenendijk & M. Stokhof (Eds.), **Amsterdam Papers on Formal Grammars**. The Netherlands: University of Amsterdam, 1976.

Fillmore, C.J. On the Syntax of Preverbs. **Glossa**, 1967, **1**, 91-125.

Garvey, C., Caramazza, A. and Yates, J. Factors Influencing Assignment of Pronoun Antecedents. **Cognition**, 1974, **3**(3), 227-244.

Geach, P. **Reference and Generality**. New York: Cornell University Press, 1962.

Grice, H.P. Logic and Conversation. In P. Cole and J. Morgan (Eds.), **Syntax and Semantics Vol. 3: Speech Acts**. New York: Academic Press, 1975.

Grinder, J. & Postal, P. Missing Antecedents. **Linguistic Inquiry**, 1971, 2(3), 269-312.

Grosz, B. **The Representation and Use of Focus in Dialog Understanding**. Doctoral dissertation, University of California at Berkeley, 1977. (Also Technical Note 151, SRI International, Menlo Park CA, July 1977.)

Hankamer, J. **Constraints on Deletion in Syntax**. Unpublished doctoral dissertation, Yale University, 1971.

Hankamer, J. On the Non-cyclic Nature of WH-clefting. In Lagaly, Fox & Bruck (Eds.), **Papers from the Tenth Regional Meeting of the Chicago Linguistic Society**, Universty of Chicago, Chicago IL, 1974.

Hankamer, J. & Sag, I.A. Deep and Surface Anaphora. **Linguistic Inquiry**, 1976, **7**(3), 391-428.

Hendrix, G. Human Engineering for Applied Natural Language Processing. **Proceedings of 5-IJCAI**, 22-25 August 1977, 183-191.

Hintikka, J. & Carlson, L. Pronouns of Laziness in Game-theoretical Semantics. **Theoretical Linguistics**, 1977, **4**(1/2), 1-30.

Hobbs, J. Pronoun Resolution (Research Report 76-1). New York: Department of Computer Science, City College, City University of New York, 1976a.

Hobbs, J. A Computational Approach to Discourse Analysis (Research Report 76-2). New York: Department of Computer Science, City College, City University of New York, 1976b.

Hughes, G. & Cresswell, M. **An Introduction to Modal Logic**. London: Methuen Publishing Co., 1968.

Jackendoff, R. **X Syntax: A Study in Phrase Structure**. Cambridge MA: MIT Press, 1977.

Kaplan, D. Quantifying In. **Synthese**, 1968-69, **19**, 118-129.

Kaplan, J. The Variability of Phrasal Anaphoric Islands. In S. Mufwene et al. (Eds.), **Papers from the 12th Regional Meeting of the Chicago Linguistic Society**, University of Chicago, Chicago IL, 1976.

Karttunen, L. Pronouns and Variables. In R. Binnick et al. (Eds.), **Papers from the Fifth Regional Meeting of the Chicago Linguistic Society**, University of Chicago, Chicago IL, 1969.

Karttunen, L. Discourse Referents. In J. McCawley (Ed.), **Syntax and Semantics** (Vol. 7). New York: Academic Press, 1976.

Karttunen, L. Whichever Antecedent. Unpublished ms. Department of Linguistics, Universiy of Texas at Austin.

Keenan, E. Names, Quantifiers and Sloppy Identity Problem. **Papers in Linguistics**, 1971, **4**(2).

Kuno, S. Some Properties of Non-Referential Noun Phrases. In R. Jakobson and S. Kawamoto (Eds.), **Studies in General and Oriental Linguistics**. Tokyo, Japan: TEC Company Ltd., 1970.

Kuno, S. Lexical and Contextual Meaning. **Linguistic Inquiry**, 1974, 5(3), 469-477.

Kuno, S. Three perspectives in the Functional Approach to Syntax. In Grossman, San & Vance (Eds.), **Papers from the Parasession on Functionalism**. Chicago, IL: Chicago Linguistics Society, 1975.

Kuno, S. Subject, Theme and the Speaker's Empathy: A re-examination of relativization phenomena. In C. Li (Ed.), **Subject and Topic**. New York: Academic Press, 1976.

Lakoff, G. Counterparts, or the Problem of Reference in Transformational Grammar. In Harvard Computation Laboratory Report NSF-24, 1970, 23-36.

Langacker, R. Pronominalization and the Chain of Command. In D. Reibel & S. Schane (Eds.), **Modern Studies in English**. New Jersey: Prentice-Hall, 1966.

Lasnik, H. Remarks on Co-reference. **Linguistic Analysis**, 1976, **2**, 1-22.

Lehnert, W. Human and Computational Question Answering. **Cognitive Science**, 1977, **1**, 47-73.

Macnamara, J. Cognitive Basis of Language Learning in Infants. **Psychological Review**, 1967, **79**, 1-13.

Maratsos, M. The Effects of Stress on the Understanding of Pronominal Co-reference in English. **Journal of Psycholinguistic Research**, 1973, 2(1), 1-8.

McCawley, J. Meaning and the Description of Language. **Kotoba no Uchu**, 1967, **2**. (Also in McCawley, J. (Ed.) **Grammar and Meaning**, Tokyo: Taishukan Publishing Company, 1973.)

Medema, P., Bronnenberg, W.J., Bunt, H.C., Landsbergen, S.P.J., Scha, R.J.H., Schoenmaker, W.J. & van Utteren, E.P.C. PHLIQA1: Multilevel Semantics in Question-answering. **American J. of Computational Linguistics**. Microfiche 32, 1975.

Montague, R. Universal Grammar. In R.H. Thomason (Ed.), **Formal Philosophy**: Selected papers of Richard Montague. New Haven CT: Yale University Press, 1974.

Mourelatos, A. Events, Processes and States. Presented at the Brown University Conference on Tense and Aspect, Department of Linguistics, Brown University, 14-15 January 1978.

Nash-Webber, B.L. Inference in an Approach to Discourse Anaphora. (CSR-77) Center for the Study of Reading, U. of Illinois and Bolt Beranek and Newman Inc., 1977. (Also in M. Stein (Ed.), **Proceedings of NELS-8**. Amherst: University of Massachusetts, 1977.)

Nash-Webber B.L. & Reiter, R. Anaphora and Logical Form: On Formal Meaning Representations for English. (CSR-36) Center for the Study of Reading, U. of Illinois and Bolt Beranek and Newman Inc., 1977. (Also in **Proceedings of 5-IJCAI**, 22-25 August 1977, 121-131. To appear in **Artificial Intelligence**.)

Newell, A. & Simon, H. GPS, A Program that Simulates Human Thought. In E.A. Feigenbaum & J. Feldman (Eds.), **Computers and Thought**. New York: McGraw Hill, 1963.

Norman, D. & Rumelhart, D. **Explorations in Cognition**. San Francisco CA: W.H. Freeman, 1975.

Olson, D.R. Language and Thought: Aspects of a Cognitive Theory of Semantics. **Psychological Review**, 1970, **4**, 257-273.

Partee, B.H. Opacity, Coreference and Pronouns. In G. Harman and D. Davidson (Eds.), **Semantics of Natural Language**. The Netherlands: D. Reidel, 1972.

Postal, P. On So-called 'Pronouns' in English. In D. Reidel & S. Schane (Eds.), **Modern Studies in English**. New Jersey: Prentice-Hall, 1966.

Postal, P. Anaphoric Islands. In R.I. Binnick et al. (Eds.), **Papers from the Fifth Regional Meeting of the Chicago Linguistic Society,** University of Chicago, Chicago IL, 1969.

Reinhart, T. **The Syntactic Domain of Anaphora.** Unpublished doctoral dissertation, Department of Foreign Literatures and Linguistics, MIT, 1976.

Reiter, R. An Approach to Deductive Question-Answering. (BBN Report 3649). Cambridge MA: Bolt Beranek and Newman Inc., 1977.

Rieger, C.J. **Conceptual Memory.** Unpublished doctoral dissertation, Stanford University, Department of Computer Science, 1974.

Rosenberg, S. Discourse Structure. (Working Paper 130). Cambridge, MA: MIT Artificial Intelligence Laboratory, 1976.

Ross, J.R. **Constraints on Variables in Syntax.** Unpublished doctoral dissertation, Massachusetts Institute of Technology, 1967.

Ross, J.R. Guess Who. In R.I. Binnick et al. (Eds.), **Papers from the Fifth Regional Meeting of the Chicago Linguistic Society,** University of Chicago, Chicago IL, 1969.

Rumelhart, D. & Ortony, A. Representation of Knowledge. In R. Anderson, R. Spiro & W. Montague (Eds.), **Schooling and the Acquisition of Knowledge.** Hillsdale, N.J.: Lawrence Erlbaum Associates, 1977.

Sag, I.A. **Deletion and Logical Form.** Unpublished doctoral dissertation, Department of Foreign Literatures and Linguistics, MIT, 1976.

Schank, R. & Abelson, R. Scripts, Plans & Knowledge. **Proceedings of 4-IJCAI,** August 1975, Tbilisi, Georgia, USSR.

Searle, J.R. **Speech Acts.** London: Cambridge University Press, 1969.

Smith, B. Levels, Layers and Planes: The framework of a system of knowledge representation semantics. Master's thesis, MIT Artificial Intelligence Laboratory, 1978.

Steedman, M.J. Verbs, Time and Modality. **Cognitive Science,** 1977, **1,** 216-234.

Vendler, Z. **Linguistics in Philosophy.** Ithaca NY: Cornell University Press, 1967.

Waltz, D. and Goodman, B. Writing a Natural Language Data Base System. **Proceedings of 5-IJCAI,** 22-25 August 1977, 144-150.

Wasow, T. **Anaphoric Relations in English.** Unpublished Doctoral Dissertation, Department of Foreign Literatures and Linguistics, MIT, 1972.

Wasow, T. Problems with Pronouns in Transformational Grammar. Unpublished ms., Department of Linguistics, Stanford University, 1976.

Watt, W.C. Habitability. **American Documentation**, 1968, **19**, 338-351.

Wilks, Y. A Preferential, Pattern-seeking Semantics for Natural Language. **Artificial Intelligence**, 1975, **6**, 53-74.

Williams, E. Discourse and Logical Form. **Linguistic Inquiry**, 1977, 8(1), 101-140.

Winograd, T. **Understanding Natural Language.** New York: Academic Press, 1972.

Woods, W.A. What's in a Link: Foundations for Semantic Networkds. In D. Bobrow & A. Collins (Eds.), **Representation and Understanding.** New York: Academic Press, 1975.

Woods, W.A. Semantics and Quantification in Natural Language Question Answering. (Technical Report 3687) Cambridge MA: Bolt Beranek and Newman Inc., 1977.

Woods, W.A. & Brachman, R.J. Research in Natural Language Understanding - Quarterly Technical Progress Report No. 1. (Technical Report 3742) Cambridge MA: Bolt Beranek and Newman Inc., 1978.

Woods, W.A., Kaplan, R.M. & Nash-Webber, B.L. The Lunar Sciences Natural Language Information System: Final Report. (Technical Report 2378) Cambridge MA: Bolt Beranek and Newman Inc., 1972 (NTIS No. N72-23155).

Woods, W.A., Bates, M., Brown, G., Bruce, B., Cook, C., Klovstad, J., Makhoul, J., Nash-Webber, B., Schwartz, R., Wolf, J., & Zue, V. Speech Understanding Systems: Final Technical Progress Report - 30 October 1974 through 29 October 1976. (Technical Report 3438) Cambridge MA: Bolt Beranek and Newman Inc., 1976.